British Appeasement and the Origins of World War II

PROBLEMS IN EUROPEAN CIVILIZATION SERIES

British Appeasement and the Origins of World War II

Edited by
R. J. Q. Adams
Texas A & M University

D. C. HEATH AND COMPANY
Lexington, Massachusetts Toronto

Address editorial correspondence to:

D. C. Heath and Company
125 Spring Street
Lexington, MA 02173

Acquisitions Editor: James Miller
Production Editor: Andrea Cava
Designer: Alwyn Velásquez
Photo Researcher: Wen-Wen Chen
Production Coordinator: Charles Dutton
Permissions Editor: Margaret Roll

Cover: Interfoto Pressebild Agentur. Chamberlain returning from Munich to Prague.

Published simultaneously in Canada.

Printed in the United States of America.

International Standard Book Number: 0-669-33502-9

Library of Congress Catalog Number: 92-76114

10 9 8 7 6 5 4 3 2

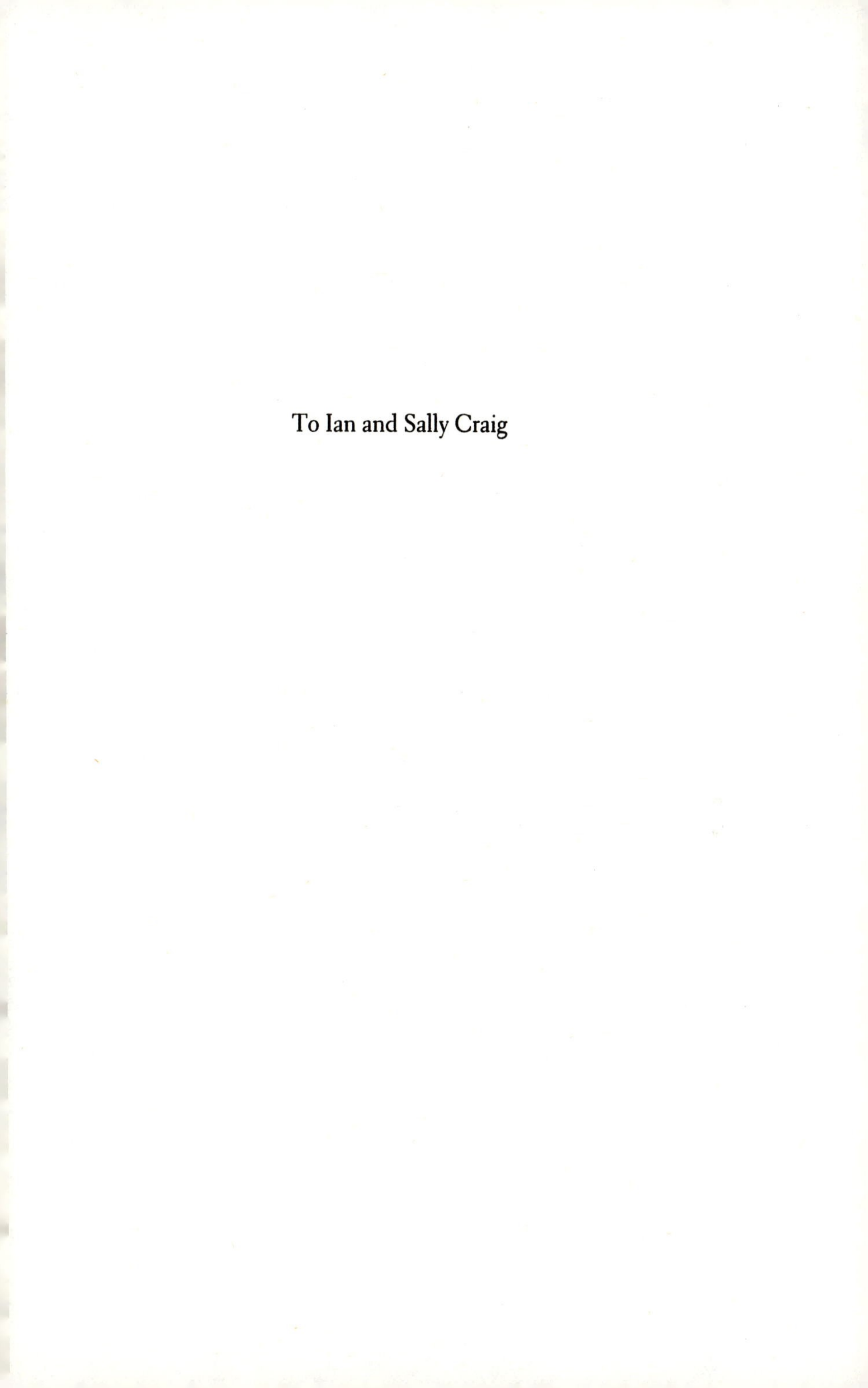

To Ian and Sally Craig

Preface

The initial shots in the continuing historical battle over the question of appeasement were fired virtually as that policy collapsed and Europe tumbled into what was to become the Second World War. Once the war was ended, hardly a month has passed without the publication of a book or article or pamphlet or, more recently, a film suggesting that the final interpretation was on offer. There seems to be no end to this powerful trend, and quite frankly, this is no bad thing. Appeasement is one of the great topics of twentieth-century British and European history, and it is altogether fitting that historians continue to examine and explain it and mine it for all its treasures of knowledge.

The collection that follows is an attempt to offer a cross-section of the major interpretations of British appeasement in the 1930s. There are also several primary sources—including the often overlooked Munich accords themselves—to give the reader something beyond historical interpretation.

The editor and publisher have strenuously labored to ensure that these selections are accurately presented. In some cases, portions have been excised by the editor in order to keep the volume within its prescribed length.

When one presents a new book to the scholarly community it is customary to offer thanks to many who helped make the publication of the work possible. This is more than mere good manners, as no one ever produced a history in solitude. My first thanks are to the historians whose works are reproduced here and to those who hold copyright to these materials for permission to publish them. In this regard, I am especially pleased to acknowledge my gratitude to Dr. B. S. Benedikz and the library of the University of Birmingham, Great Britain, for permission to publish Neville Chamberlain's letter reproduced in Part III. I am grateful also to the reviewers who offered useful comments and criticisms of this collection, namely Catherine A. Cline, Catholic University of America; Nicholas C.

Edsall, University of Virginia; Fred M. Leventhal, Boston University; and Peter T. Marsh, Syracuse University. Thanks also are due to James Miller and Andrea Cava of D. C. Heath and Company, whose help in this project from beginning to end was invaluable. My wife, Susan Charlotte Adams, was, as usual, a source of good counsel and invaluable support. I wish to record my thanks to the Texas A & M University Faculty Development Program and the TAMU Military Studies Institute for assistance while I prepared this collection. I am grateful also to the Master and Fellows of St. Catherine's College, Oxford, who facilitated my work by electing me to a visiting fellowship. Ian Craig and Sally Craig of that same great and ancient seat of learning have been a constant help over the years, and I could not contemplate the writing of British history in America without them. It is to these good friends that I dedicate this volume.

R. J. Q. Adams

Contents

Chronology of Events

1931	October 27	National Government wins general election
1932	March 23	Stanley Baldwin tells Parliament "the bomber will always get through"
1933	January 30	Adolf Hitler becomes Chancellor of Germany
1934	January 26	German-Polish Nonaggression Treaty signed
	March 7	British Defense Requirements Committee recommends rearmament in face of potential Japanese and German threats
	March 8	Baldwin declares Britain will not be inferior to any nation in air power
	May 29	World Disarmament Conference ends in failure
	August 2	Death of German President Paul von Hindenburg Hitler combines offices of president and chancellor to become Fuhrer of Germany
1935	March 4	First White Paper on Defense calling for rearmament
	March 9	Goering announces existence of German Luftwaffe
	March 16	Hitler announces 36-division army and conscription
	April 11–14	Stresa Conference
	May 2	Franco-Russian Mutual Assistance Treaty signed
	June 7	Baldwin becomes prime minister for the third time

	June 18	Anglo-German Naval Treaty signed
	October 3	Italy attacks Abyssinia
	November 18	General election won by National Government
	December 8	Hoare-Laval Pact initialed in Paris
	December 18	Eden succeeds Hoare as foreign secretary
1936	March 1	Sir Thomas Inskip appointed first minister for Coordination of Defense
	March 3	Second White Paper on Defense
	March 7	Hitler remilitarizes Rhineland
	July 17	Spanish Civil War begins
	November 1	Rome-Berlin Axis announced
1937	January 2	Anglo-Italian Gentlemen's Agreement signed
	April 29	Nevile Henderson becomes British ambassador to Germany
	May 28	Neville Chamberlain succeeds Baldwin as prime minister
	November 5	"Hossbach Conference" of Hitler and German high command
	November 6	Italy joins Anti-Comintern Pact of Germany and Japan
	November 19	Lord Halifax meets Hitler
	December 15	Inskip reports on defense program and recommends emphasis on air power, limited expenditure, and home defense over continental commitments
1938	January 11	Chamberlain rejects President Roosevelt's peace initiative plan
	February 20	Eden resigns; Halifax becomes foreign secretary
	March 12	Hitler carries out *Anschluss* with Austria
	March 28	Chiefs of staff report to the cabinet inability of British forces to aid Czechoslovakia in case of German invasion

	April 21	Hitler and his generals agree on Opera tion Green for the destruction of Czechoslovakia
	April 24	Sudeten leader Konrad Henlein makes public his "Karlsbad Demands" against Czech government
	May 19–22	May Crisis Britain warns Germany against military invasion of Czechoslovakia
	August 28	Chamberlain reveals to his closest advisors his "Plan Z" to fly to Germany to meet with Hitler
	September 5	Czech President Edvard Benes agrees to majority Karlsbad Demands; Henlein rejects Czech offer
	September 7	Editorial in The Times advocates cession of Czech Sudetenland to Germany
	September 15	Chamberlain flies to Germany for talks with Hitler in Berchtesgaden
	September 23	Chamberlain meets Hitler a second time in Godesberg
	September 25–6	Anglo-French conference in London
	September 27	Chamberlain appeals to Mussolini to intervene with Hitler and prevent war
	September 28	Hitler agrees to conference with Britain, France, and Italy
	September 30	Munich conference
	October 1–10	German troops occupy Sudetenland
1939	January 11–14	Chamberlain and Halifax visit Mussolini in Rome
	February 27	Britain recognizes Franco regime in Spain
	March 15	German troops march into Prague as Czechoslovakia ceases to exist
	March 22	Lithuania cedes Memelland to Germany
	March 30	Britain guarantees Poland

Principal Proper Names

Baldwin, Stanley: British Prime Minister, 1935–1937.
Beck, Col. Jósef: Polish Foreign Minister, 1932–1939.
Benes, Edvard: President of Czechoslovakia, 1935–1938.
Bonnet, Georges: French Foreign Minister, 1938–1939.
Butler, Richard Austen ("Rab"): Undersecretary of State for Foreign Affairs, British Foreign Office, 1938–1941.
Cadogan, Sir Alexander: Permanent Undersecretary of State for Foreign Affairs, British Foreign Office, 1938–1946.
Chamberlain, Neville: British Prime Minister, 1937–1940.
Churchill, Winston: British Member of Parliament, 1900–1963.
Cooper, Alfred Duff: British Secretary of State for War, 1935–1937; First Lord of the Admiralty, 1937–1938.
Daladier, Edouard: French Minister of National Defense, 1936–1938; French Premier, 1938–1940.
Eden, Anthony: British Foreign Secretary, 1935–1938.
Goering, Reichsmarshal Hermann: Commander in Chief of the Luftwaffe, 1935–1938.
Hacha, Emil: President of Czechoslovakia, 1938–1939.
Halifax, Edward, Third Viscount: British Foreign Secretary, 1937–1940.
Henderson, Sir Nevile: British Ambassador to Germany, 1937–1939.
Hitler, Adolf: German Chancellor and Fuhrer, 1933–1945.
Hore-Belisha, Leslie: British Secretary of State for War, 1937–1940.
Hoare, Sir Samuel: British Foreign Secretary, 1935; First Lord of the Admiralty, 1936–1937; Home Secretary, 1937–1939.
Inskip, Sir Thomas: British Minister for the Coordination of Defense, 1936–1939.
Litvinov, Maxim: Soviet Commissar for Foreign Affairs, 1930–1939.

MacDonald, James Ramsay: British Prime Minister, 1924; 1929–1935.

Masaryk, Jan: Czech Ambassador to Great Britain, 1925–1939.

Molotov, Vyacheslav: Soviet Commissar for Foreign Affairs, 1939–1956.

Mussolini, Benito: Italian Premier and Duce, 1922–1943.

Neurath, Constantin Freiherr von: German Foreign Minister, 1932–1938.

Paul-Boncour, Joseph: French Premier, 1932–1933; French Foreign Minister, 1933–1934.

Phipps, Sir Eric: British Ambassador to Germany, 1933–1937; to France, 1937–1939.

Ribbentrop, Joachim von: German Foreign Minister, 1938–1945.

Roosevelt, Franklin D.: President of the United States, 1933–1945.

Runciman, Walter Viscount: British Liberal politician; led Runciman Mission to Czechoslovakia, 1938.

Simon, Sir John: British Foreign Secretary, 1931–1935; Home Secretary, 1935–1937: Chancellor of the Exchequer, 1937–1940.

Swinton, Phillip Viscount: British Secretary of State for Air, 1935–1938.

Stalin, Joseph: General Secretary of the Central Committee of the Soviet Communist Party, 1922–1953.

Vansittart, Sir Robert: Permanent Undersecretary of State for Foreign Affairs, British Foreign Office, 1930–1938.

Wilson, Sir Horace: Chief industrial advisor to the British government, 1930–1939; advisor to Prime Minister Chamberlain.

Wood, Sir Howard Kingsley: British Secretary of State for Air, 1938–1940.

Variety of Opinion

Appeasement was Chamberlain's policy, above all others:

> *Chamberlain was a shy autocrat and made his own policy in silence before he made it Cabinet policy. If appeasement began as a common Cabinet policy, it was he who gave it such an emphasis as to add a pejorative sense to the word. I can, moreover, find no example in two and a half years of Cabinet meetings in which the discussions in Cabinet altered his mind on a subject. . . .*
>
> Ian Colvin

Appeasement was a noble effort, regardless of the result:

> *We know from the Nuremberg trial documents that Hitler was insatiable, war inevitable and appeasement therefore a forlorn hope. But since those who pursued appeasement lacked the benefit of hindsight, it was neither a foolish nor an ignoble hope. The case for appeasement thus rested on the proposition, not merely that it would have been folly to incur war without adequate defenses or reliable allies, but morally wrong to accept it as inevitable unless every attempt had been made to redress legitimate grievances peacefully.*
>
> Iain Macleod

Appeasement was the safe middle ground:

> *For twenty years at least, and arguably much longer, the British political nation had tended to agree that a cheap, pacific, non-interventionist foreign policy suited the national interests. Appeasement was the course favored by public opinion; it represented the "middle ground," so secure against the impracticalities of the left and the right; and it was the means whereby Lloyd George, Baldwin, MacDonald and Chamberlain himself could bolster up their domestic positions and supervise Britain's economic recovery.*
>
> Paul Kennedy

The Munich agreement was a triumph for the British way of life:

> *It was a triumph for all that was best and most enlightened in British life; a triumph for those who had preached equal justice between peoples; a triumph for those who had courageously denounced the harshness and short-sightedness of Versailles.*
>
> A. J. P. Taylor

The roots of appeasement ran deep in British history:

> *If we apply some of these [research] habits to the history of appeasement, and not merely to the years 1935 to 39, we shall discover that its roots go deep into the past; that the forces at play were formidable and intractable; that Hitler had no simple catalogue of aggression; and that it is unhistorical and unjust, and therefore wrong both in the factual and in the moral senses of the word, to heap the blame on the predilections and the follies of a few.*
>
> David Dilks

Chamberlain foolishly believed Hitler:

> *When Mr Chamberlain stepped out of his airplane on the return from Munich, he said, "This means peace in our time."*
>
> *After he got back to Downing Street he shouted from the window, "I bring you Peace with honor." He also remarked, "Out of this nettle, danger, we pluck this flower, safety."*
>
> *Nobody can accuse Mr. Chamberlain of being a willful liar. He said those things because he believed them. He was absolutely satisfied that when Hitler signed that little piece of paper, the heart of a man who had built up his regime by treachery, lies and deception, had changed.*
>
> "Cato"

Appeasement was the product neither of stupidity or weakness:

> *Appeasement after 1935 was not a passive reactive policy but an active pursuit of peace among the European Great Powers by men who were convinced that they possessed the only realistic formula to achieve that noble goal. It is also true that this approach failed. Whatever else might be said, it must always be remembered that the appeasers did not pursue a course which led to such tragic results because they were weak or cowardly or stupid or wicked; whatever the reasons, what they were was wrong.*
>
> R. J. Q. Adams

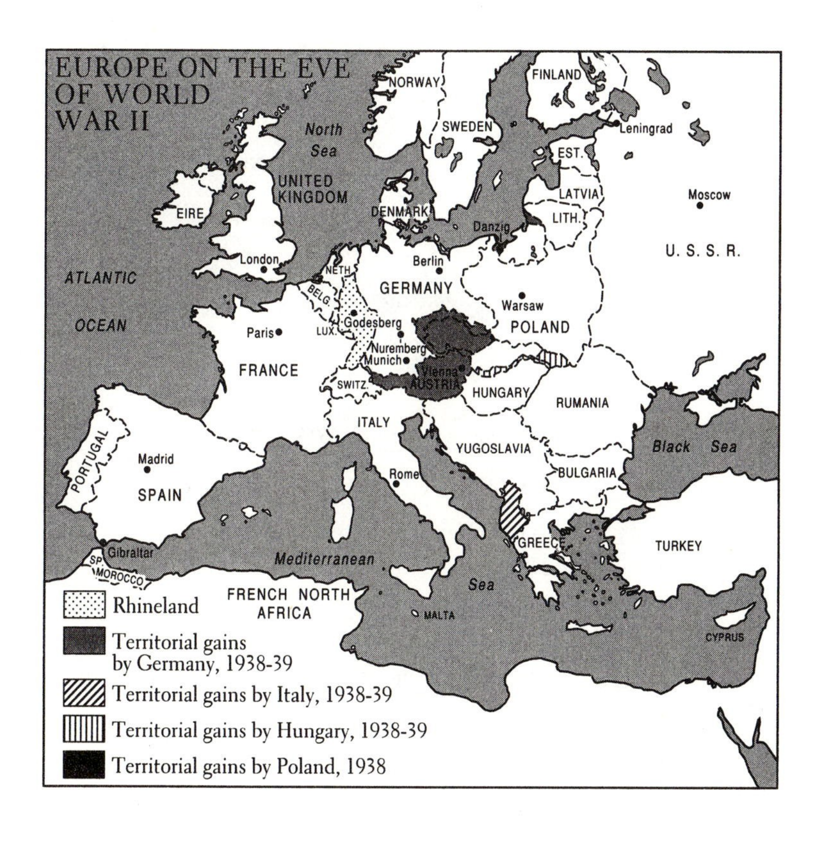
EUROPE ON THE EVE OF WORLD WAR II
NORWAY
FINLAND
SWEDEN
Leningrad
North Sea
EST.
UNITED KINGDOM
LATVIA
Moscow
EIRE
DENMARK
LITH.
Danzig
U. S. S. R.
London
NETH.
Berlin
ATLANTIC
BELG.
GERMANY
Warsaw
OCEAN
Godesberg
Paris
LUX.
POLAND
Nuremberg
Munich
FRANCE
Vienna
AUSTRIA
SWITZ.
HUNGARY
RUMANIA
ITALY
PORTUGAL
Madrid
YUGOSLAVIA
Black Sea
SPAIN
Rome
BULGARIA
GREECE
TURKEY
Gibraltar
SP.
MOROCCO
Mediterranean Sea
FRENCH NORTH AFRICA
MALTA
CYPRUS
Rhineland
Territorial gains by Germany, 1938-39
Territorial gains by Italy, 1938-39
Territorial gains by Hungary, 1938-39
Territorial gains by Poland, 1938

AUSTRIA, CZECHOSLOVAKIA, AND POLAND, 1938-39

- German Anschluss with Austria, March 1938
- Sudetenland: Annexed by Germany, October 1938
- Southern Slovakia: Annexed by Hungary, October 1938
- Těšín: Annexed by Poland, October 1938
- Protectorate of Bohemia and Moravia: Occupied by Germany, March 1939
- Slovakia: Nominally independent, March 1939
- Subcarpatian Ukraine: Annexed by Hungary, March 1939
- Memelland: Annexed by Germany, April 1939
- Danzig: Annexed by Germany, September 1939
- Polish territory annexed by Germany, September 1939
- Polish territory annexed by U.S.S.R., September 1939

Introduction

There is no such thing as an inevitable war. If war comes it will be from failure of human wisdom.

The British statesman Andrew Bonar Law spoke these words before the coming of World War I, a conflict that was to raise him to a position of great power but would cost him two beloved sons. Few historians today would insist that a great war was inevitable in 1914, and all have much to say about the degree of human wisdom in place in the European capitals in the first fourteen years of the twentieth century.

In regard to the Second World War, both notions—inevitability and the wisdom of statesmen—remain controversial. Was another major war predestined, given the foreign policy goals of the Hitler regime in Germany after 1933 and the mind-set of the European leaders who opposed him? Furthermore, would the latter and greater conflict have been avoided had the leadership of the other Great Powers—particularly Britain and France—been wise enough to read the signs before them and take certain clear steps to prevent it? All participants in such debates point to the policy of appeasement and to the Munich agreements of 1938 as key matters in this controversy. Though France played a significant role, as in their own ways did the United States, the self-governing British dominions, and the Soviet Union, the active appeasement of Germany (and, to a lesser degree, of Italy) was primarily a British phenomenon. These matters—questions and suggested answers— provide the unifying theme of the following collection.

In the years following 1919, war-weary Britain sought a Europe that was balanced militarily, politically, and economically. The Peace of Paris, especially the Treaty of Versailles with Germany, was never popular in Britain because of its perceived harshness toward a Germany that remained—even in defeat—inexorably the greatest continental power and a desirable trading partner. A wounded, vengeful, and anxious France seldom found the British enthusiastic partners in their drive for a permanently weakened Germany.

The desire for a peace based on international balance remained strong in Britain, but the outlook for achieving such a permanent system grew increasingly gloomy as the years following the Peace of Paris unfolded. The League of Nations, formed without the membership of either the United States or the Soviet Union, was a disappointment in guaranteeing peace; and the Locarno Pact of 1925 seemed for only a short while a suitable substitute. The year 1922 saw the advent of the first fascist dictator, Benito Mussolini. After 1933, the new Nazi Fuhrer shortly came to be seen as a far greater danger to peace than his fellow dictator, surpassing the Italian in both rhetoric and sheer menace.

Hitler, like the less offensive leaders of the Weimar Republic he had destroyed, was dedicated to the destruction of the noisome clauses of the Versailles treaty. Shortly after coming to power he made public his plans to that end. In early 1935, the Fuhrer announced what the world's intelligence services already knew: that he was building a sizable air force and meant to build a large army based on military conscription—both forbidden under the terms of the Versailles pact. In the same month Britain, the only European Great Power to take seriously her disarmament vows made at the peace conference, reluctantly announced a program of limited rearmament.

The crises that Winston Churchill was later so persuasively to interpret as the clear steps to world war came quickly thereafter. The autumn of 1935 saw Mussolini's unprovoked invasion of Abyssinia (modern Ethiopia) and the advent of growing difficulties for a Britain wishing in vain to retain Italian good will (and separation between the fascist powers) while, at the same time, upholding at least the semblance of opposition to blatant military aggression. The increasingly dangerous climate for peace led to divisive and protracted arguments in Britain, in this time of world economic depression, over the degree and cost of the proposed rearmament that had now become necessary.

March 1936 brought another crisis as Hitler, despite the collective opposition of his generals, unilaterally remilitarized the Rhineland in clear violation of the terms of Versailles. The former victor powers, Britain and France, protested but did not act. The Rhineland was German territory, and the democracies would not take action to prevent Hitler from, in the popular phrase of the day, "going into his own back garden."

The following year saw the accession to the British premiership of the sixty-eight-year-old Neville Chamberlain. The famous son of a famous father, Chamberlain hated war and considered the horror of 1914–1918 a mistake that must not be repeated. He had waited many years to gain the first place in British political life, and his goal was to remove the possible causes of war through the peaceful settlement of the reasonable grievances of a Germany badly treated at Paris in 1919.

Fateful 1938 began ominously as in March, Hitler made good on his goal to join his native Austria to the German Reich. Also expressly forbidden by Versailles, the so-called *Anschluss* was once again met by the democracies only with protests.

The absorption of Austria made all but inevitable a crisis involving Czechoslovakia, which at the peace conference had been granted territory in its western provinces containing more than three million ethnic Germans. After the *Anschluss*, the expanded Reich bordered that region, the Sudetenland, on three sides. This problem—what to do with the ethnic German minority in Czechoslovakia—took its place at the center of the policy that came to be known as appeasement. A Britain governed by men who hated war, who knew that their rearmament was incomplete, and who sympathized to a degree with Germany's complaints against the 1919 peace, ultimately was represented (with France, Italy, and Germany) at the controversial meeting in Munich in September 1938 in which the western frontiers of Czechoslovakia were reshaped—without, it should be noted, serious consideration of the wishes of that small democracy. The Sudetenland passed to Germany, and Hitler was denied nothing except the glory of a victorious war.

It soon became obvious to all that Munich did not purchase "peace for their time." In March of 1939, and in spite of his promises six months earlier at Munich, the Fuhrer brutally dismembered the rest of Czechoslovakia. Hitler, further convinced that the democracies would never fight, turned his demands toward the hated Polish Corridor and the city of Danzig—taken from the Reich, once again, at Versailles.

Convinced at last that Hitler could not be trusted, Britain and France reluctantly prepared to resist. Chamberlain warned the dictator that, although negotiation was still possible, military aggression would surely lead to European war. In his own hand, Chamberlain drafted a military guarantee to Poland, followed shortly thereafter by similar guarantees to other smaller powers in the path of Hitler's grandiose ambitions. The summer saw belated and ultimately fruitless negotiations with the Soviet Union in search of broadening the anti-Hitler bloc. On September 1, undeterred, the Fuhrer struck against Poland; Britain declared war two days later. What would become World War II had begun.

The significance of appeasement within the tradition of British foreign policy in the nineteenth century is examined by Paul W. Schroeder in the first selection in this book. Was appeasement a departure from the traditions of British foreign relations, or were Chamberlain and his colleagues simply pursuing a policy that had worked well for Britain in the days of her greatest power? If so, how and why did it go wrong?

To understand the decisions made by Britain's leaders, it is useful to understand something of the climate of opinion of their time. The first selection in the second part is by Martin Gilbert, from his book *The Origins of Appeasement*, and concerns British perceptions of Germany in the years following the Peace of Paris. How much of appeasement policy, it might be asked, grew not from fear of Germany but from the popular opinion that that great nation had legitimate complaints about her treatment after her defeat?

Gustav Schmidt, in the next reading, raises the issue of the often overlooked significance of domestic concerns in the making of foreign policy. What political, economic, and other internal matters were on the minds of the appeasers as they attempted to deal with Hitler? What was the British political "agenda" in these times of economic depression, and why did it make it necessary to avoid, if possible, the expense of all-out rearmament?

The other offering in this section is from an essay by Michael Howard, who discusses the position of the British military high command and the factors that influenced defense planning in the appeasement period. In light of this and the preceding essay, what were the realities of and limitations on British military preparation with which her high command had to deal?

The next part of the collection deals with the crises confronting the British government in this period, forever condemned by Churchill as the "years the locust hath eaten." The first of these, from *Munich: The Price of Peace* by Telford Taylor, deals with the 1935 Italian invasion of Abyssinia. According to Taylor, Britain attempted a "double policy" of bluff and conciliation in regard to Mussolini's Italy, which ultimately failed totally. With this in mind, how can the disastrous Hoare-Laval pact be explained and understood?

The next selection is from Maurice Cowling's *The Impact of Hitler: British Politics and Foreign Policy, 1933–1940* and presents an analysis of British reactions to the remilitarization of the Rhineland in 1936. From this interpretation, what can be learned about the foreign policy of Anthony Eden, who is usually favorably contrasted with the appeasers at this time, and about Anglo-French relations in 1936?

Larry William Fuchser, in an excerpt from his *Neville Chamberlain and Appeasement*, next presents the view that British policy toward the German-Austrian *Anschluss* essentially marked the end of any hope for Czechoslovakia. How were these two events, the *Anschluss* and the Czech crisis, linked, and what was learned (or not learned) in early 1938 by each side—German and British—about the other? Further, according to Fuchser, an unalloyed critic of Chamberlain, what insights into the thinking of the new prime minister can be gained from his response to these events?

Finally in this part are two primary sources: the first is a private letter from Neville Chamberlain to his sister, written on March 20, 1938, revealing his judgment that realistically there was little Britain could do to aid Czechoslovakia in case of German invasion. The second is taken from the minutes of the conference between French and British leaders held in London on April 28–29, 1938, following the *Anschluss* crisis. It makes clear that the democracies intended to use all influence possible over Czechoslovakia to cause that small nation to settle the Sudetenland crisis with Germany, and that Britain, though willing to warn Germany about the danger of making war, was unwilling to offer any promise of assistance to their French colleagues should they honor their guarantee to Prague. In light of the revelations in these documents, what choices were open to the democracies? Was the Czech crisis settled before Munich?

Part IV deals with the Munich crisis itself, and the first offering is the radio speech of Neville Chamberlain broadcast on September 27, 1938, when war seemed terrifyingly probable. What is to be learned about the prime minister's view of the value for Britain of resisting Hitler's threats against the Czechs—a quarrel between "people of whom we know nothing"?

Next is the description given in the diary of Harold Nicolson of the high drama in the House of Commons as Chamberlain received and read aloud Hitler's invitation to the Munich conference. This dramatic telling makes very clear the near unanimity of support Chamberlain enjoyed at this moment.

The next two selections give contrasting contemporary views of the results of Munich: the first, from Stuart Hodgson's *The Man Who Made the Peace*, published immediately following the conference, gives some understanding of the adulation heaped on the prime minister by his many admirers for weeks afterward. The second consists of portions of perhaps the best of the many anti-appeasement philippics of Winston Churchill: his speech in the House of Commons debate over the Munich agreements, held on October 5, 1938. In light of the usual criticism aimed at the appeasers, these brief excerpts offer some understanding of the controversial nature of Munich at the time. It should be recalled that, at the time, Hodgson's view was far more popular than Churchill's.

Last in this section is the text of the Munich accords themselves, followed by the famous "piece of paper": the brief agreement Chamberlain extracted from the Fuhrer and later held aloft for reporters and newsreel cameras when he returned to Heston Aerodrome after the conference. Was the prime minister naive to think that any peace, much less peace for their time, was possible?

The single entry in Part V details the change of course of British policy after the German seizure of the rump of Czechoslovakia in March 1939 and is again by Telford Taylor. What, one might inquire, was accomplished by the guarantees to Poland and other small states and the prolonged negotiations with the Soviet Union? Perhaps more importantly, especially in light of the fact that it did not prevent war, what is to be learned from this change of course, coming as it did and when it did?

The next part of the collection is given over to the question of understanding appeasement and those who practiced it. The first selection is by Sidney Aster, an assessment of the traditional or "Guilty Men" interpretation of the appeasers—that they were culpable for failing in their duty to keep their country secure.

A different view may be gained from Roy Douglas's interpretation, from his *In the Year of Munich*, that Chamberlain played what was essentially an impossible hand and played it as well as could be expected.

In an excerpt from what is perhaps—after three decades—still the most controversial book on the subject, *The Origins of the Second World War*, the late A. J. P. Taylor argues that appeasement, rather than deserving the criticism it has received, was in fact a policy that was both realistic and, to a degree, even enlightened.

To conclude Part VI, Paul Kennedy offers a thoughtful criticism of both the defenders and critics of appeasement policy, and Keith Middlemas, in the selection from his *The Strategy of Appeasement*, gives an unemotional analysis of the major mistakes committed by the appeasers—errors which in his view made any hope of success impossible. The views of the critics and counter-critics found in this section aid our understanding both of the difficulties and the misperceptions of the appeasers. They also shed light on the differences that exist among historians on the difficult matter of explaining appeasement.

The sole offering in Part VII, by Christopher Layne, offers an analysis of the significance—the lesson and the burden—of appeasement and the Munich crisis for U.S. policymakers in a time when the Cold War is fading away, to be replaced by other international concerns. It should be noted that this was written before the collapse of the Soviet Union and the recent Gulf War. The collection ends, then, on what is perhaps the most used and misused question in contemporary discussions of Munich: What is to be learned?

THE OLD-FASHIONED CUSTOMER

"I wonder if you've got a song I remember about not wanting to fight, but if we do . . . something, something, something, . . . we've got the money too?"

March 1938: In the aftermath of the *Anschluss*, an anti-appeasement John Bull seeks from Chamberlain a more "traditional" British foreign policy. (From *Punch* 3/23/38. Historical Pictures/Stock Montage, Inc.)

PART

Appearement in the British Context

Paul W. Schroeder

Munich and the British Tradition

Paul Schroeder, professor of history at the University of Illinois at Urbana-Champaign, explores not the usual questions about appeasement—of motives and causes—but asks "what kind of policy it was . . . and how it is best understood in a generic rather than a genetic sense." He posits that appeasement thinking did not represent a departure from traditional British foreign policy, that instead it "conformed to the standard nineteenth-century British approach to central and East European problems."

From "Munich and the British Tradition," *The Historical Journal* (Great Britain) 19, 1 (1976), pp. 223–243. Reprinted by permission of Cambridge University Press.

Despite more than thirty-five years of scrutiny, the British policy of appeasement in the 1930s continues to be the subject of discussion and controversy. The search for explanations of Munich has even been intensified in recent years by the opening of the Cabinet papers. This essay does not pretend to make any contribution to the study of the "causes" of Munich—the motives and determinants of British policy—or to decide the issue between the "guilty men" and the "terrible times" schools of explanation. Instead of asking what caused British policy in the 1930s, it asks what kind of policy it was, i.e. into what class or category of policies it properly falls, with what kinds of action it can usefully be compared, and how it is best understood in a generic rather than a genetic sense.

This question is not plucked from the air. It has been sometimes explicitly asserted, often implicitly assumed, that appeasement represented a deviation from normal British policy in the nineteenth and early twentieth centuries, indeed, in most of modern times: the maintenance of a balance of power in Europe, the prevention of Continental hegemony by any one Power, the protection of the independence of smaller states, the discouragement of the use of force and the overthrow of treaties. The assumption that appeasement represented a shift in British policy, a departure from the norm, may be plausibly supposed to have contributed to the intensive search for explanations of it, and to the supposition that the explanations are to be found in Britain's changed situation after World War I. The thesis of this essay is that Munich did not represent a departure from tradition, but rather conformed to the standard nineteenth-century British approach to Central and East European problems.

In dealing with a subject so much discussed as Munich, it is easy to give the impression that one has just discovered America. This thesis is not the same as others which it may apparently resemble. It does not argue that the roots of British appeasement of Germany already show up early in World War I, as Martin Gilbert points out. Nor does it contend, like A. J. P. Taylor, that appeasement belongs to the general dissenting tradition of British foreign policy. Nor does it follow Corelli Barnett in viewing appeasement as the result of Britain's abandoning a healthy, realistic eighteenth-century concept of power politics in favour of Gladstonian moralism and internationalism in the nineteenth century. The argument here is rather that appeasement represented a continuation of standard nineteenth-century British policy in Europe, in a sense its culmination; that the policy of appeasement was essentially the same as the policy (supposed or so-called) of maintaining the balance of power in Europe.

It is plainly impossible to expound and back up this thesis thoroughly, defending it against all the possible objections to it, within the scope of a brief essay. All that will be attempted here is a general comparison of the two policies on their main points. One can best begin by comparing the basic assumptions of appeasers in the 1930s as to what Britain's overall policy towards Europe and the world should be, with those of nineteenth-century British statesmen. The appeasers believed that Britain should not give alliances or direct commitments except to the Low Countries and France. Her primary attention must still be given to the Commonwealth and Empire and to world trade. Armaments expenditures had to be maintained at a level compatible with sound finances and a strong British economy. If war became unavoidable, Britain ought to concentrate on naval, air, and commercial warfare, leaving the large-scale fighting on land to her allies. She ought to retain as free a hand as possible in European and world affairs, leading and controlling her allies, France in particular, so that Britain would not become entangled in other peoples' quarrels.

One needs, I think, only to state these views to recognize them as the standard outlook of nineteenth-century Britain, very slightly modified to meet twentieth-century conditions.

The same point can be made, though it is less immediately obvious, when one compares the thought of the appeasers with that of their nineteenth-century forebears in particular regard to Central and Eastern Europe. The appeasers recognized as fundamental the fact that a unified nationalist German state existed whose size, resources, geographical location, and industrial development inevitably made her the leading power in Central Europe, and on the whole they approved of this state of things. A reasonably strong and prosperous Germany served to curb the Soviet Union, check hegemonic aspirations and dangerous initiatives on the part of France, and promote European and British prosperity. The appeasers also recognized that the large numbers of ethnic Germans living outside Germany's 1919 frontiers would probably (perhaps inevitably) some day want to join the Reich. Whether such an *Anschluss*, in Austria and elsewhere, would prove beneficial to Europe, a source of greater stability, or dangerous, depended upon whether the problem was ultimately settled by force or by peaceful means. In any case, Britain had no grounds for interfering with this natural historic development. Instead, she should use her example, friendship, and good advice to encourage Germany to pursue her legitimate ends by peaceful means, at the same time urging the states east and south-east of Germany, whom Britain and her allies in any case could not defend, to seek a peaceful settlement with Germany quickly, while concessions might still prove mutually advantageous.

Once again, these are all standard nineteenth-century British ideas and attitudes. Although Britain never officially promoted German unification, the idea that German nationalism was on the whole a force for good, that Germany needed to be unified, and that Prussia was best suited to lead in the process, gained currency in Britain surprisingly early. Already in 1841, at a time when Britain and Austria were not opponents but allies cooperating closely in the Eastern Question, Palmerston predicted the ultimate victory of Prussia over Austria in Germany. British statesmen, especially Whigs, showed a clear preference for greater German unification under Prussian leadership during the 1848 revolutions, and even more so in the opening stages of the Crimean War and during William I's initial years as prince-regent and king of Prussia. Strong British criticisms of Prussian policy in 1849–50 and 1854–6, and even more bitter denunciations of Bismarck in the 1860s, do not really change the picture. No matter how angry the British might be at Prussia's attacks on Denmark or failure to fight Russia, or disappointed at her defections from liberalism and constitutionalism, or outraged at Bismarck's methods, they continued to recognize Prussia as the natural and desirable leader and unifier of Germany and to deal with her on this basis—just as Chamberlain did not allow his genuine dislike of Hitler and Germans to blind him to the necessity of good relations with Germany. Even the emergence of serious Anglo-German rivalry at the turn of the century made no essential difference in the British attitude. British leaders might oppose Germany's naval and colonial policies, fear her ambitions, resent her rivalry in trade, and dislike her manners, but they never seriously considered trying to undermine her domination of Central Europe. Far from attempting, for example, to encourage Austro-Hungarian independence from Germany and trying to use Austria-Hungary to check German power in Central Europe, the British counted on Germany's control over Austria-Hungary and encouraged it in order to prevent a war over the Balkans. Even during World War I, there was surprisingly little sentiment in Britain for a partition of Germany or a drastic territorial reduction that would destroy her Central European power position.

It might be objected that nineteenth-century Britain accepted and welcomed only the "Little Germany" of Bismarck, with its historic rather than nationalist basis and its explicit renunciation of Great German or Pan-German goals, while Chamberlain at Munich accepted Great German aims and opened the door to Pan-German expansionism. The distinction will not stand examination. More than once in the nineteenth century Britain faced a clear and imminent prospect that Great Germany might come into being, and showed no concern over it. In 1866 it seemed possible, even probable, to British observers as well as others, that the Austrian Empire would break up, with at least its German and Czech provinces being absorbed into a unified Germany led by Prussia. Neither Clarendon, foreign secretary when the war began, nor Stanley, who succeeded him while it was under way, showed any anxiety over this possibility or developed any policy to meet it. Though some British leaders felt a sentimental regret at Austria's apparent demise, the sole practical concerns entertained in London were that British nonintervention might be destroying Britain's prestige on the Continent, or that the general territorial scramble ensuing on Austria's breakup might result in territorial gains for France. This latter consideration mainly explains the British pressure on Austria to make peace quickly with Prussia, even if it cost Austria dearly.

Although Austria secured a temporary lease of life in the Peace of Prague, Stanley, who viewed the new alliances of the South German states with the North German Confederation as a healthy development leading towards their inevitable absorption into Germany, continued to assume that Austria's German provinces would also take the same route sooner or later. Not everyone in Britain (especially not Clarendon) was as complacent about this as Stanley, but they fully shared his conviction that there was nothing Britain could or should do about developments in Central Europe. Hence the British welcomed Germany's victory over France in 1870–1 not only because it eliminated the danger to Britain from France, but also because it solved the Austrian and Central European problem in Bismarck's way, which Britain approved: it forced Austria to seek her security in the protection of a powerful Germany. In the same spirit, Salisbury greeted the Dual Alliance of 1879 as good tidings of great joy. But when after 1895 even German protection seemed no longer able to arrest the course of Austrian internal decay, and Frenchmen, Russians, Serbs, and others began planning for the contingency of the Empire's breakup on the death of Francis Joseph, the British steadily refused to concern themselves with the question, even though plainly such a development would promote the formation of a Greater Germany, including at least German Austria, probably also Bohemia-Moravia, and possibly even Carniola and Istria.

Thus there is no reason to doubt that the British would have accepted a Greater Germany in 1848–9, 1866, 1871, or before World War I just as readily as they did in 1938. But perhaps there is a real difference between accepting a Greater Germany when one cannot prevent it (as the nineteenth-century British believed they could not) and trying to establish lasting peace by means of partnership with a Great Germany, as Chamberlain hoped to do. In fact, here too Chamberlain thought and acted strictly within the British tradition. His father Joseph had actually strayed from that tradition a bit in seeking a formal alliance with Germany in 1898–1900. Neville Chamberlain merely wanted what many nineteenth-century statesmen wanted: a "natural alliance" with Germany, an informal working partnership for peace based on similar interests and harmonious aims.

Again, when the appeasers contended in the 1930s that the West should not encourage Austria and Czechoslovakia to offer armed resistance to Germany, because the West could not support them effectively and resistance would only lead to their destruction, while timely concessions to Germany might gain Austria and Czechoslovakia her friendship and support, this British policy and advice followed (doubtless unconsciously) good nineteenth-century precedents. To cite only one parallel, after 1866 British leaders repeatedly urged Austria to accept her defeat and to ally herself with the new North German Confederation against Russia, warning her that it would be disastrous to try to compete any longer in Germany or to try to check Prussia by an alliance with France.

While all this may show that the ideas and assumptions of appeasement are rooted in the British tradition, it does not answer the more important question whether the appeasers really acted as British statesmen traditionally had done. The answer to this question requires again a quick review of what the appeasers did. First, they declined to enforce the disarmament provisions of Versailles (even where these were confirmed at Locarno),* accepting a rapid build-up of the German army, while trying by negotiations to curb German weapons that directly menaced Britain. Thus the British reacted only mildly to Germany's reintroduction of conscription and the remilitarization of the Rhineland, while putting considerable effort into reaching a naval pact and trying for an air pact with Germany.

The appeasers further decided, even before Germany made any overt move against Austria or the Sudeten territories, that Britain could not undertake any commitments over these areas unless a conflict arising out of them escalated and directly involved British interests in the West. Thus they ignored or downgraded the strategic importance of these lands for Czechoslovakia, France, Poland, and other countries. This stance further meant in effect (though not intent) encouraging Germany to turn eastward against the Soviet Union. At Munich, Chamberlain participated directly in the revision of treaties and the redrawing of international boundaries under the threat of force, in order to satisfy an aggressive, powerful state at the expense of a smaller,

*The nonaggression pact signed in 1925 between Germany, France, and Belgium, guaranteed by Britain and Italy, reiterating the western territorial provisions of the Versailles Treaty.

weaker one, without granting the loser either new effective guarantees or other territory as compensation. Britain further helped settle this great European question without including either the victim, Czechoslovakia, or one of the Great Powers directly involved, the Soviet Union, in the negotiations.

These decisions and actions do seem inconsistent with the nineteenth-century British tradition, and help account for the feelings of shock and shame still occasionally expressed in writings on Munich. But the break with tradition is more apparent than real. Just as she did in the 1930s, it was normal for nineteenth-century Britain to pay little attention to Continental armies, and to respond sharply only to a possible naval threat. The hegemonic threat of the Russian army of Nicholas I, the French army of Napoleon III, or the Germany army of Bismarck and William II all disturbed Britain far less than the navies which each of these powers built or contemplated building.

It was equally normal and traditional, as has already been shown, for Britain to concede that all of East Central Europe fell into Germany's sphere. As for pushing Germany eastward against the Soviet Union, Chamberlain's policy on this score was not nearly so deliberate and overt as that of nineteenth-century Britain, which repeatedly tried to turn Germany's and Austria's attention and ambitions to the east against Russia. To be sure, only once, during the Crimean War, did the British try to promote a Russo-German war and to encourage German and Austrian territorial ambitions at Russia's expense. At other times they merely wanted to encourage the German powers to guard against Russian expansion and domination. This was equally Chamberlain's aim. He too simply wanted to encourage Germany to play her natural role of bulwark against Russia, without encouraging German expansionism or war.

Nor was it a new departure for Britain at Munich to exclude either a smaller power or a great power from the settlement of an issue vital to them. Canning went over Austria's head to settle the Greek question first with Russia alone, and then with Russia and France; Britain helped impose a solution drawn up by the three allies on Turkey by force; Palmerston effectively excluded the Netherlands from the negotiations establishing Belgian independence. At Britain's insistence, Prussia was excluded from the Crimean War peace conferences of 1855 and 1856, while Russia was shut out even after the war's end from decisions regarding the Danubian Principalities and the protection of Christians in Turkey. Britain repeatedly tried to push through her programme for liberating Italy in partnership with France or with France and Sardinia alone, excluding Austria and the independent Italian states, especially Naples and the Papal states. The Macedonian reform programme which Britain worked out with Russia in 1907–8 was intended to push Austria to one side; the Entente Cordiale of 1904 was designed to turn Morocco and Egypt, for decades major international questions, into affairs which Britain and France alone would decide. Even the reasons Chamberlain could give for not bringing the Soviet Union into the arrangements for Czechoslovakia were traditional: Russia was not trustworthy, not even really a European power. Other powers would be alienated if she were brought in, or her participation might promote a continental league that could trap Britain in an undesirable settlement or unwelcome commitments.

One thing still may seem unique about Munich, however: Chamberlain's co-operation with an aggressive Great Power in tearing up treaties and signing away a smaller power's territory without compensation. Surely nineteenth-century Britain upheld the sanctity of treaties and defended the independence and integrity of smaller states?

No doubt one can make a case for this contention. The British claimed without successful contradiction that they had never violated a European treaty, and on various occasions, notably over the annexation of Cracow in 1846, over the denunciation of the Black Sea clause of the Treaty of Paris in 1870, and over the annexation of Bosnia in 1908, they protested strongly against unilateral denunciation or revision of treaties by others. However, the question in 1938, as the appeasers saw it, was not whether Britain should break a treaty binding on her (there was no direct British commitment to Czechoslovakia), but whether she and her allies should risk a great war in order to defend a particular treaty and particular territorial boundaries. On this issue, Chamberlain's policy stands firmly in the British tradition: that of seeking the peaceful revision of treaties, and refusing to go to war even when treaties were overthrown by force if that war would be futile or counterproductive. Through most of the nineteenth century, Britain had sided not with those who wished to maintain the Vienna treaty system intact, but with those who wanted to revise it; sometimes she was on the side of those who openly attacked it and tried to destroy it. Platonically or actively, she had at various times encouraged and aided the Greeks, the Belgians, the Italians, the Germans, the Rumanians, the Bulgarians, the Serbs, the Montenegrins, and the Macedonians to overthrow the *status quo*. The arguments the British used to justify this were precisely those of Munich: that the old order was outworn and untenable, that general peace was the overriding consideration, and that changes now would lead to greater peace and stability in the long run.

Admittedly, Britain had some record in the nineteenth century of defending smaller states and of standing by victims of aggression. Belgium and Sardinia afford the best examples of this, but Turkey, Portugal, Switzerland, and Denmark also at times benefited from British intervention and protection. Yet the British did not defend, or even favour, the independence and integrity of *all* smaller states and victims of aggression, especially not in Central Europe. The British strongly approved of the extinction of the independence of Parma, Modena, Tuscany, the Two Sicilies, and the Papal States, despite the fact that their absorption into Italy involved clear violations of international law. Britain did not even pursue diplomatic efforts to save Hanover, Nassau, Electoral Hesse, and Frankfurt in 1866, and passed by the absorption of the independent states of South Germany into Germany in 1870–1 without a word. Nor was it unprecedented that Britain should in 1938 combine with a more powerful state to impose losses upon a weaker one. This was precisely the technique Palmerston and Russell proposed in January 1860 to solve the Italian question. Though they considered France to be basically aggressive and a serious danger to the balance of power, and knew that Austria after her recent defeat was particularly vulnerable and threatened, they proposed making an alliance with France and Sardinia to impose Anglo-French-Sardinian terms upon Austria, if necessary by force. To be sure, French annexation of Nice and Savoy soon led Palmerston and Russell to want to use Austria and Prussia to check France, and even to consider allying with them against her. But no long-range commitment to defend Austria as a part of such an arrangement was considered. The sole purpose was to use the German powers to stop French expansion, and by the end of the year Russell was back to contemplating a general European combination against Austria to compel her to give up Venetia. Palmerston and Russell always claimed, doubtless genuinely, to be pursuing laudable goals in any such scheme: to limit French ambitions and gains, to settle the dangerous Italian question once and for all, to preserve general peace, and incidentally to help Austria by disembarrassing her of a discontented and ungovernable province. *Mutatis mutandis* [with due alteration of details], this is precisely what Chamberlain sought to do by co-operation with Germany in 1938. To take another example, prior to World War I Britain regularly sided with Russia against a weaker power, Austria, knowing that Russia's policy was expansionist, but reasoning, among other things, that Russia was bound to win out over Austria in the long run anyway.

Even the style of appeasement reminds one in many ways of nineteenth-century British methods. When one observes British reactions to the crises of the 1930s, particularly 1938—refusing to make plans in advance for future contingencies, insisting upon maintaining a free hand until the crisis actually developed, intervening to offer British mediation or good offices when the situation appeared to become critical, telling both sides that with a little mutual goodwill the issue could readily be resolved, repeatedly warning both opponents not of what Britain might do, but of what other powers might do if they did not compose their quarrel—one is almost irresistibly reminded that she employed these same diplomatic techniques before the Danish-German war, the Austro-Prussian war, the Franco-German war, and other crises in the nineteenth century. Similarly, when the British urged the Czechs to make major concessions to Germany, contending that these would actually improve Czechoslovakia's position and insisting that this was friendly advice from a well-wisher, while at the same time they declined to assume any obligations toward Czechoslovakia if she made the desired concessions, they were employing the same kind of language and tactics as Britain used toward Austria in Italian and Balkan questions. If the appeasers seemed to ignore the danger that Czechoslovakia would undermine her own existence by granting Sudeten German claims, British statesmen had earlier seemed equally unaware what it would do to the Austrian Empire to admit the nationality principle in Italy, Hungary, or elsewhere. (Actually, in both cases the British to some extent recognized the likely results, but this was not enough to constitute a deterrent.) Chamberlain's or Nevile Henderson's belief that the Czechs could make friends of Germany by timely concessions is not much different from the common nineteenth-century British belief that a little friendly treatment from Austria could turn Italians or Serbs into friends and allies.

Even in its economic aspects, appeasement reminds one in certain ways of nineteenth-century aims and attitudes. That is, while economic appeasement was clearly an attempt to meet particular twentieth-century British economic problems (just as political appeasement was designed to meet particular political and military problems), it still represented a kind of continuation of the common nineteenth-century belief that increased trade between Britain and the Continent, especially Germany, would help overcome national rivalries and promote peace.

There is an answer that might be made to this thesis, reading somewhat as follows: comparisons and parallels such as these prove very little. Nothing is more dangerous in history than to argue from analogy, nothing more obvious than that circumstances alter cases. Where the parallels are valid, they merely prove the unsurprising point that some factors influencing British policy over the centuries have remained constant—geography, resources, certain basic interests. Moreover, whatever one thinks about the alleged analogies, the thesis as a whole involves two grave, crippling distortions of British history. It first ignores some critical occasions in the nineteenth century where Britain clearly did not follow an appeasement policy, most notably the Crimean War and 1914, when Britain accepted war rather than endure Russian or German hegemony in Europe. It further treats nineteenth-century British policy as a uniform whole, ignoring the plain fact that British policies and attitudes towards Europe were sometimes active and interventionist, sometimes passive and isolationist. To judge from this thesis, one would suppose that British policy was the same whether it was being run by Aberdeen or Palmerston, by Disraeli and Salisbury or by Gladstone and Granville, by Grey or Morley—as peculiar a view as supposing that it would have made no difference in 1938 had Churchill been premier instead of Chamberlain.

These are important objections. They must not merely be countered in order to defend the thesis, but answered in such a way as to make clearer the purpose of comparing appeasement to the nineteenth-century tradition—to demonstrate, if possible, the heuristic value of the exercise, the additional understanding of both policies which it may yield.

As to the first point, British policy in 1853–6 was certainly not one of appeasement. It was rather one of preventive war. In so far as the Crimean War had a clear purpose for Britain (it certainly had for Palmerston), that purpose was not to save Turkey, prevent Russian aggression, or check Russian hegemony in Europe. All these dangers, to the extent that they had really existed, were curbed or ended before the war began. The purpose was to throw Russia back, reduce her power, eliminate her as a threat to Britain and Europe for some decades. This policy of confrontation and preventive war differs not only from Munich, but from all the rest of nineteenth-century British policy towards Europe as well. There may have been other British preventive wars in the world but no other was ever seriously contemplated against a European power. Even if this point were not considered important enough to make the Crimean War an exception to standard nineteenth-century British policy rather than an instance of it, the basic question would still remain: Did British policy in 1853–6 really differ from Chamberlain's where it most counted, in Central Europe? On this, more later.

As for British policy in 1914 and before, it was the same as Chamberlain's. In both cases Britain hoped to avoid war while preserving a general balance of power in Europe; in both she was ready to cede Central Europe to German domination, but hoped to contain her by co-operating (short of close alliances) with the powers on Germany's flanks. In each case Britain was committed to the defence of the Low Countries and France, but determined not to fight over a quarrel in Eastern Europe or the Balkans. Only the circumstances differed, not the policy. Had Germany in 1938 invaded Belgium or declared war on France, Chamberlain would have gone to war just as Asquith did in 1914. Had Austria-Hungary been able to occupy Serbia bloodlessly in 1914 as Germany occupied Austria in 1938, or had only a localized Austro-Russian war developed out of the 1914 crisis, there would have been even less inclination for Britain to intervene then than there was in 1938. Both policies rested on the same basic assumption: that the general European balance of power which Britain needed and wished to maintain could be upheld without much regard to the particular system of relations or territorial arrangements obtaining in Central and South-eastern Europe. Chamberlain's policy presupposed that even if Germany dominated or absorbed Czechoslovakia, some form of Anglo-French co-operation with Eastern European states could still hold the balance. Grey's policy presupposed that there would still be a European balance acceptable to the West even if Germany and her satellite Austria-Hungary succeeded in dominating the Balkans politically, economically, and militarily, or, conversely, if Russia succeeded in defeating and breaking up Austria-Hungary and establishing her domination of the Balkans.

This indicates the answer to the objection that this thesis distorts traditional British policy by levelling out crucial differences within it, ignoring the distinctions between activism and quietism, intervention and isolation, appeasement and resistance to aggression. The answer is that this thesis does not require one to view nineteenth-century British policy as a single uniform whole in all respects, nor does it ask that one accept at face value alleged resemblances between appeasement and nineteenth-century policy which might be matched by counter-examples, or analogies and comparisons which might be regarded as misleading. The thesis does require that nineteenth-century British policy be seen as a uniform whole in one essential respect; that there be a major element common to, and essential to, both appeasement and the whole nineteenth-century tradition; that the analogies and comparisons become meaningful and valid in respect to this element; and that the divergent tendencies within British policy, however important otherwise, do not make a substantial difference in respect to it.

That essential element is the basic British conception of Central Europe's role in the European system, of how Central Europe should be organized for that role, and of its importance to Britain. This British conception, already indicated in part, needs to be reviewed a bit more systematically.

As everyone knows, nineteenth-century British statesmen frequently referred to the German powers as natural allies of Great Britain, essential to the European balance of power. They meant by this that the German powers served British interests by filling a power vacuum, checking France and Russia, and thus helping to preserve general peace. It was to the end (or least on the ostensible grounds) of helping to make Central Europe sufficiently strong, stable, and united to carry out this task that the British tried to promote liberal constitutional government, free trade, and concessions to nationalism in Central Europe. The long British campaign to get Austria first to sponsor reforms in Italy, and later to abandon Italy to the Italians, fits into this same scheme; Italy kept Austria and Germany from being strong where it counted, north of the Alps. The same reasoning accounted for British acceptance and endorsement of Bismarck's *Reich*, despite the violent and illiberal means by which it was created and governed. The British had concluded long before 1866 that a Prussian-led Germany would be stronger and more progressive, and thus a better check on France and Russia, than Austria or the old German Confederation had been. The frequent British denunciations or suspicions of Austria and Prussia for a servile attitude toward France or Russia, and the consistent British concern to break up or nullify combinations like the Holy Alliance, the Three Emperors' League, or Franco-Austrian or Franco-Prussian alliances, fit into the same pattern. Insufficient vigilance by the German powers against Russia and France tended to undermine the balance of power, and could even lead to a Continental league against Britain.

Thus the European system as the British conceived it presupposed a basic conflict between all the actors, each jealously guarding its independence, and especially a conflict and balance relation between Central Europe and the two flanks. Hence the oft-expressed British concern lest internecine quarrels between the German states distract and weaken them in the face of France and Russia, and the relief in Britain which greeted final German unification in 1871. Now the whole area was solidly organized, and Austria, secure under German protection and no longer tempted to flirt with France, would be free to check Russia in the East. As for Britain, she could continue her traditional policy of promoting the independence of all states, turning their natural rivalries to her own interests and those of civilization and progress, and in general supporting the German powers in their balancing role.

The European system as Britain conceived it was thus mechanical in operation. No organic relation connected the system with the existence of any particular actor; there only needed to be enough states sufficiently determined to preserve their own independence to balance each other off. Nor was any particular organization of Central Europe vital, so long as the essential balancing function was being carried on. Hence the British could accept and approve the great changes in the Central European system from mid-century on, without sensing in this any inconsistency with their view of Prussia and Austria as Britain's "natural allies." They could even usually support nationalist causes in Central and South-eastern Europe so long as these did not play into Russia's hands or damage British Near Eastern interests, without feeling that they were helping to undermine Central Europe as an element in the balance of power. For any number of states could play in the balancing game—generally speaking, the more the better, and the more nationally satisfied the participants were, the more stable and capable of guarding their independence they would be. Hence the frequent optimistic British assertions that a united Italy, Greece, Rumania, or Bulgaria, or even a resurrected Poland, would easily fit into the European balance and play a useful role in it.

What this implies is that, for all the talk of a natural alliance between Britain and Austria, Prussia, or Germany, the British really felt only an indirect, contingent interest in Central Europe. Having the German powers check Russia and France was useful, serving to remove a possible direct threat to Britain from France, and to relieve Russian pressure on British interests in the Near East and elsewhere. It also helped enable Britain to hold the balance of power, intervening or staying out of European questions more or less as it suited her, and devoting most of her attention to domestic and imperial concerns. But British statesmen never recognized Central Europe as directly vital to Britain's world position in the way the Near East, the Straits, the Mediterranean, Egypt, or other areas were. Along with many of the assurances of British friendship and informal alliance given to Austria or Prussia went reminders that they needed Britain far more than she needed them. With a minimum of vigilance and preparedness, Britain could always defend her own territory and empire, making it too costly even for a coalition to attack her. Should she ever be in real danger of defeat, the Central Powers' own vital interests would force them to come to Britain's aid. Should they prove too timid, treacherous, or greedy to be relied on (which the British often felt was the case) Britain could always defend her interests through a direct deal with her opponents. Finally, if Russia and France ever ceased to be the main dangers to British interests and the balance of power, the usefulness of Central Europe to Britain would end; indeed, Central Europe could become a danger to her.

On these three major points—the conception of Central Europe as useful primarily for checking France and Russia; the concept of the balance of power as essentially mechanical and operating more or less automatically, because of the natural desire of all states for independence, irrespective of the particular territorial or political arrangements for Central Europe; and the belief that Britain had only a limited and contingent interest in Central Europe—British policy in the nineteenth century is a unified whole. British statesmen might be Austrophile or Austrophobe, friendly or distrustful toward Germany, sympathetic or unsympathetic toward nationalism, interventionist or isolationist; it made no difference so far as these ideas were concerned.

The connexion of all this with Munich is that Munich represents a last effort by Britain to make this traditional outlook work, at a time when (as before 1914) Germany appeared to be a threat rather than an informal ally. It represents, that is, a last effort to manage a Central European crisis and preserve peace in the traditional British way—by conceding to Germany wide legitimate interests and leadership in Central Europe, trying to mediate cautiously between the rival states for peace, taking advantage of the natural rivalries of Continental powers to preserve a general balance, and preserving a policy of limited commitments for Britain, with no obligation to defend any particular territorial or political arrangement in Central or Eastern Europe itself.

To argue that Munich was traditional in this sense might not seem controversial or even important. For the argument, even if granted, would only seem to illustrate anew the persistence of unexamined traditions and patterns of behaviour in history; to show once again the influence of misplaced historical memory. The mistake at Munich consisted of believing that Britain was still at the height of her nineteenth-century power, that Hitler was like William II, and that other nineteenth-century conditions still prevailed—or at all events acting as if this were so. It consisted even more in the miscalculation of other powers' policies, the refusal to recognize the unappeasable nature of Nazi and Fascist aims. The failure of appeasement therefore proves that policy which had suited British needs well in the nineteenth century was tragically unsuited to twentieth-century conditions.

This is plausible enough—indeed, it is mainly quite true—but it is not the thesis of this essay. No doubt appeasement failed because the conditions which had made British policy possible and apparently successful in the nineteenth century no longer prevailed in the 1930s. The question here raised is whether British policymakers even in the nineteenth century had been aware of what the conditions vital to British foreign policy success really were, and whether British actions in the main and over the long run had helped sustain these conditions or undermine them. No doubt appeasement represented in certain ways a lapse into illusion, from which 1939–40 brought a rude awakening. The question here raised is whether twentieth-century British policy toward Europe does not also contain a dim, partial awakening from some nineteenth-century illusions, and whether the final awakening did not come decades too late to do anything about restoring the vanished bases of British foreign policy autonomy and success.

It is plain that disillusionment with Munich set in very quickly, not only among the public but also within the government. By October and November 1938, leading foreign officials were describing Munich as a debacle, recognized that the balance of power was destroyed beyond repair, and resigned themselves to further German expansion eastwards and south-eastwards. While they differed sharply on what to do, no policy anyone could recommend offered Britain any solid prospect of security and peace. Their gloomy assessment, fully justified by events, seems to constitute a trenchant critique of appeasement. The question to be considered here is whether the grounds given for seeing Munich as a debacle do not also indicate certain fundamental inadequacies of nineteenth-century British balance-of-power policies.

Why, in traditional balance-of-power terms, was so grim a diagnosis of the situation after Munich justified? In late 1938 Germany still controlled less territory and population than she had at the outbreak of the First World War, assuming (as the British did) that Austria-Hungary was in 1914 under Germany's control. Independent European states still existed (France, the Soviet Union, Poland, Rumania, Yugoslavia) with ample potential power to curb Germany and plenty of reason on traditional balance grounds to want to do so. What kept the balance of power from working? The easy answer is, new conditions: the decline of Western power, the alienation of Russia, a power vacuum in East Central Europe, the transformation of modern warfare by new weapons, and the fact that Hitler instead of Bismarck or William II ruled Germany—all true enough, all known to the Foreign Office. Yet on close examination one sees that some of these conditions were not new or decisive, and that one needs to pinpoint the essential condition more precisely.

It was not Western power that had given Britain her ability to pursue an autonomous policy in the nineteenth century. From 1919 to 1936 (perhaps even later) the Western powers were stronger relative to the rest of Europe than they had been through most of the nineteenth century. France's divisions and internal weakness had often been proverbial, especially during the Third Republic; she and Britain had often been opponents, not allies as they were in 1938. Whatever strengths nineteenth-century Britain had boasted in her Empire, her economy, and her navy, she had been helpless to intervene effectively on the Continent without allies. If twentieth-century weapons had ended Britain's invulnerability, these weapons were available to Germany's opponents as well as to Germany, as Hitler well knew and took into account in all his plans. They enabled Britain now to get at Germany as well as Germany to get at her. Russia was no doubt a great question mark in 1938; but had she been so secure and reliable an ally in 1914 or earlier? The danger of her paralysis by internal revolt, or her defection to Germany's side, seemed as grave before 1914 as in the 1930s. Even the internal troubles which weakened the Western democracies in the 1930s were not unprecedented; Nicholson, Hardinge, and others had often wondered before 1914 if Radicalism and Irish troubles were not ruining Britain's ability to conduct foreign policy or retain her allies and empire.

The decisive factors in making it impossible for Britain to carry out her traditional policy successfully were the changes in Central Europe—the power, methods, and aims of Nazi Germany, and the chaotic conditions in East Central and South-east Europe which afforded Germany an open field for expansion. But Germany had been militarily capable of conquering this whole area since the 1860s. What had restrained her for half a century, and kept the area from being an easy target? The reasons British officials gave after Munich for their pessimistic outlook indicate a dim awareness on their part that instead of simply a general balance of power, there had been a specific system in Central Europe which had served to restrain Germany and the other powers and to preserve peace, and that Britain's most fundamental problem now was her complete inability to restore this system, substitute for it, or operate without it.

When, for example, William Strang, head of the Central Department of the Foreign Office, designated as the first factor in the weakening of Britain's position since Versailles the fact that Germany now faced a congeries of weak small states to the east and south in place of the Habsburg and Romanov empires, he was (besides stating a truism) implicitly recognizing at least two major points missing from the traditional British view. The first was that a general balance of power in Europe was of little use without a particular balance, a specific system of containment of German power, *within* Central Europe. The second was that Austria-Hungary had been more important to Britain and Europe for checking

Germany than for restraining Russia and France. Strang's further argument that Bolshevism had weakened Eastern Europe's defences against Germany by making it impossible to raise Panslavism as a counter to Pan-Germanism strikes one as rather like supposing that a city's health can be maintained by checking cholera through typhus. But at least Strang recognized the necessity of having some feasible alternative to Pan-Germanism as an organizing principle for Central Europe. Panslavism could not be it; these two racist doctrines had only helped to promote each other and to pave the way for world conflict in 1914. Neither had the nationalism of the Successor States worked as an alternative organizing idea. What had worked with some success before 1914 was the existence of a great power in the area, Austria-Hungary, which simply could not survive the triumph of either Pan-Germanism or Panslavism, and had to resist both ideologies.

Furthermore, when the British recognized the obvious fact that East Central Europe as organized after 1919 constituted not an obstacle to German (or Russian) expansion, but more an open field for it, they were implicitly recognizing two further major defects of their traditional view. The first was that small independent powers do not naturally play a useful role in the balance of power, but rather imperil it, unless their independent existence can be guaranteed by a tacit or explicit great power agreement. The second is that a sound system for Central and East Central Europe could not rest on a balance of power, with each state trying to guard its independence vis-à-vis the others. There was still ample potential power in Eastern Europe in 1938 to check Germany, and enough desire for independence; but (as the British had begun to see during World War I) it would all be useless without cohesion. No organization of East European states was really possible after 1918 that could have enabled them both to meet their individual problems and to present a united defence against their great neighbours. An alliance with France could not suffice in the long run to protect them from Germany; to throw themselves into Russia's arms was unthinkable for them.

All this points to the most important insight missing from the traditional British view: the fact that the nineteenth-century Central European system had never primarily served to fill a *power* vacuum in Europe, checking Russia and France. It had filled an ever-threatening *organizational* vacuum in Central Europe itself, combating entropy and dissolution. It had served to manage (though not to solve) the special political and racial problems of Central Europe. To do this at all, the system had to be organic, not mechanical; working by symbiotic, ecological balance, not balance of power. The primary threat that any major change in Central Europe had posed was not, as the British always supposed, to the general balance of power, but to the particular ecology of that area, to the existence of its system and its members. What sustained the Central and East Central European system was not balance-of-power politics, with Britain leaning to one side or the other at the proper moment, but shared interests, watchful alliances, grudging partnerships, the mutual reluctant acknowledgement that one's neighbours were indispensable to oneself. The instruments of the system were all reactionary devices the British disliked and opposed—the division of Poland, the Holy Alliance, Münchengrätz, the Three Emperors' League.

For the inhabitants of Central and Eastern Europe, the effects of this nineteenth-century system were, to say the least, very mixed. At best it was heavily weighted in the interest of peace and stability at the expense of progress, freedom, and justice. But for British foreign policy, this system had been unalloyed gain. If, as Donald Lammers puts it, the Munich crisis "had forced the Government to understand that it utterly lacked the means to conduct an autonomous foreign policy," we can now see that Britain's ability to conduct an autonomous foreign policy in the nineteenth century had rested squarely upon the existence of this kind of symbiotic system in Central Europe, which the British had not then understood or sustained. So long as this system served to restrain Germany and Russia from achieving or even seriously trying for the domination of Europe (Nicholas I's Russia and Bismarck's Germany had never been more than half-hegemonial), Britain could intervene in European questions, could lean to one side or the other, and it would make only a marginal difference. The basis of the autonomy of nineteenth-century British foreign policy was the fortunate irrelevance of Britain to the Central and East European system. 1914 was a dramatic proof that if this system broke down, Britain's autonomy would end and she would be dragged into a war fought basically to decide who would control East Central Europe, a question in which she had no interest. 1938–9 is further dramatic proof that without a satisfactory substitute for this nineteenth-century system (which Britain probably could not have created in 1919 or after) she could neither stop Germany or Russia from trying for European hegemony, nor stay out of the resultant conflict when it arose.

Were all this granted, what difference would it make? How could it affect our judgment of the appeasement policy and its makers? For even had they known and assented to the thesis here laid out, it could not have influenced their decisions. It is absurd to suppose that the British statesmen of the 1930s, intensely preoccupied with meeting the problems of that time, could have concerned themselves with the mistakes and misconceptions of their forebears which had supposedly helped create their dilemmas—like expecting a man desperately engaged in fighting a fire in his house carefully to consider the basic flaws in its construction which had made the fire possible.

This point is certainly correct. Therefore (to emphasize the point again) this thesis is not proposed as an explanation of Munich, but an interpretation of it—an attempt to suggest and define the continuities and deeper changes that escape the contemporary observers of great events. After all, explaining Munich in terms of what caused or motivated it is no problem. In one way it is very easy, in another impossible. The immense amount of research which has been done and is still being done on the origins and motivations of appeasement, and the controversy over these issues, is very informative and useful up to a point, but beyond it merely confusing. If one begins to tot up all the plausible motivations for appeasement—fear and horror of another war, Britain's state of military unpreparedness, fear for the British economy and the Empire, the unprepared state of public opinion, the isolationism of the Dominions and the United States, lack of confidence in France, lack of interest in Central Europe, failure to understand Hitler and Nazism, fear and distrust of the Soviet Union and Communism, the absence of a viable alternative presented either by the Conservative opposition or Labour, and more—one sees that these are far more than enough to explain it. It was massively overdetermined; any other policy in 1938 would have been an astounding, almost inexplicable divergence from the norm. Under such circumstances, it does not even help much to try to seek out the main cause or causes; when everything seems to lead toward a certain decision, it is often impossible even for the person who makes the decision to know what was the most important factor in it.

Appeasement then needs to be interpreted rather than explained, viewed synoptically as part of a larger pattern. The pattern is one of a long decline in Britain's world power and position. It has long been obvious that Munich was a symptom more than a cause of Britain's decline; that there were no good policies available to her, only a choice between evils and dangers. This does not mean that no policy was better than any other—only that the pessimistic warnings of both sides were alike true. Churchill was right in warning that the longer one waited to stop Hitler, the worse the results would be. The appeasers were right in warning that it would probably be very costly to stop Hitler in 1938. Austria and Czechoslovakia were vital to the balance of power in Europe, as a few recognized; but Austria could not be saved by Britain, Czechoslovakia would probably have been destroyed, as many contended, if the attempt had been made to save her. No real security system against Germany could be constructed without the Soviet Union, as Churchill insisted. But the Soviet Union was never really available to the West as a loyal partner ready to bear the main brunt of a land war, as Western strategy would demand of her. Ultimately the unchecked growth of German power menaced the British Isles directly, as the anti-appeasers had warned. But the economic and political consequences of British victory over Germany in another great war were to prove almost as damaging to Britain's world position as those of defeat , as the appeasers had feared.

The point of advancing this thesis, then, is not to blame appeasers for foolishly clinging to an outmoded tradition, still less to gloat over Britain's impasse in 1938 or to disparage the courageous resolution to fight in 1939 and 1940. It is rather simply to bring out a neglected deeper reason why Britain faced such cruelly narrow choices in the late 1930s: that fact that appeasement, a normal policy of conciliation and avoidance of war based upon a traditional balance-of-power outlook, was attempted at a time when a symbiotic system in Central and East Central Europe which had made that traditional policy apparently successful had long since disappeared, and when Britain could no longer do anything to replace it or substitute for it. If it has any validity, this view must serve to turn some attention away from the luckless policymakers at Munich and concentrate it rather upon their fortunate nineteenth-century predecessors, who succeeded with the aid of a system they never really understood, much less created or sustained; who more than once ran the risk of seeing this system smashed, and of having dangers for Britain akin to those of the 1930s arise, and who passed through it all with little policy or action, sometimes without even knowing that risks had been run. There may be no lessons at all to be learned from Munich, especially no moral lessons. But if there are, one suspects that they are the perennial ones of all history—that the sins of the fathers are visited upon the children unto the third and fourth generation; that the fathers have eaten sour grapes, and the children's teeth are set on edge.

December 1937: According to the cartoonist David Low, Chamberlain and Halifax attempted to balance British policy toward Hitler between the two extremes of their party. (From *Evening Standard* 12/10/37. e.t. archive)

PART

The Climate of Opinion

Martin Gilbert

Nostra Maxima Culpa

Many in Britain were appalled at the excesses of the Nazi regime that came to power in Germany in January 1933. Martin Gilbert, author of the latter volumes of the massive official biography of Winston Churchill, argues that despite this abhorrence, many influential Britons continued to be hopeful that Germany could be restored as a satiated friendly partner. These appeasers, as they came to be called, believed that Germany had been wronged at Versailles, and that Hitler wished only to lead his people to a renewed self-respect achievable through the meeting of their legitimate grievances against the 1919 peace settlement.

From *The Roots of Appeasement*, pp. 142–150, reprinted by permission of A P Watt, Ltd.

Before Hitler came to power, it was easy to be in favour of Anglo-German co-operation. Reasons for appeasement were varied. Four stood out most clearly. Firstly, there was the belief in a special Anglo-German affinity, of the sort of which Joseph Chamberlain had spoken, whose origins went back to the days when Angles and Saxons set off in their wattle boats from the mouths of the Rhine, and paddled with the tide towards the Humber, the Wash, and the Thames; a racial unity born before Christ in the mists of legend; a unity of blood which a shared royal dynasty had strengthened in recent times; a belief in a close cultural association, in mutual understanding in the heady realms of philosophic speculation and artistic creation. To accept such a belief needed little mental effort, and only a modicum of self-deception. Secondly, belief in a shared Anglo-German responsibility in the outbreak of war—a belief fostered by British historians and encouraged by German propaganda, casting doubt upon the morality of Britain's action in 1914, and leading to the question: "Could Britain, by a different foreign policy, have averted an Anglo-German clash?" This disturbing question, if answered in the affirmative, led those that had asked it directly on to a search for a new foreign policy that would make a repetition of 1914 impossible. Thirdly, appeasement seemed justified by the alleged severity of Versailles, a Treaty which was now seen as the "inevitable" parent of German bitterness and Nazi triumph. Fourthly, appeasement sprang from the desire to find an alternative to a pro-French policy; from fear that France would use Britain as a catspaw to keep Germany weak; and from fear that too close a partnership with France would commit Britain to a permanent policy of encirclement—permanent until Germany, in desperation, chose to break the ring of hostile states by force. Why should Britain participate again in this unfair hampering of natural and legitimate German aspirations? Why should a sentimental attachment to France force Britain into a position where she shunned collaboration with her virile North Sea neighbour? And thence, by a short and nimble jump, one was back with the Angles and Saxons preparing to embark for their island home over a thousand years before. To these arguments Nazism added one more: the need to check communism. This made a strong impact in Britain. It was the basis of a new lease of life for appeasement, temporarily discredited by Nazi tyranny.

Hitler himself claimed to be acting as the principal guardian of Europe against the spread of communism. Although the danger of a communist crusade against capitalist Europe had been averted by the Polish defeat of the Bolshevik armies in 1920, Hitler claimed that the danger was still a serious one. Many Englishmen believed him; and in answer to those who asked how we could possibly side with one tyranny against another, they answered that the evils of communism were eternal, but that the evils of Nazism could be killed by kindness. Fear of communism, and the belief in Nazism's ultimate reformation, were powerful new assets to the appeasement argument. From 1933–7 they helped to sustain a substantial body of British opinion, and to muddle official thinking at a time when a clear head, a sharp mind, and an honest tongue were more than ever needed by British policy makers.

The new appeasement fed on ignorance. People who had no clear idea about the internal conditions of Germany believed in Hitler's claim that all he wanted for Germany was to restore her self-respect. Those who heard stories of concentration camp brutality were often inclined to attribute them to exaggerated rumours. Among those who controlled national newspapers were some who did not scruple to leave out anti-German material if their policy happened to be rapprochement with Germany. Geoffrey Dawson, Editor of *The Times*, went further, even seeking news items that might show the Germans how eager he was for good relations. "I spend my nights," he wrote to Lord Lothian, as late as 1937, "taking out anything which I think will hurt their susceptibilities, and in dropping in little things which are intended to soothe them." Lothian himself acted as an independent proponent of the German viewpoint, writing constantly to friends, to the Press, and to critics explaining why appeasement was both sensible and moral, and likely to be effective in preventing the return of war. Lord Lothian was encouraged in his beliefs after a talk with Hitler himself. The two men found that they had much in common. As lapsed Catholics they were able to share an anti-Papal joke. Both feared what they considered the ever-present danger of communism in western Europe, a communism that both believed would not grow naturally, but would spread across Europe by Russian intrigue. Both insisted that the territorial provisions of the Versailles Treaty should be revised. Both considered that Anglo-German friendship was an essential factor in persuading Europe to accept "peaceful change." Lothian's views were strengthened by his meeting with Hitler. But they were views held independently and tenaciously. It would be a mistake to think that Hitler hypnotized his many English visitors into accepting his point of view. The majority of those visitors were converted before they arrived. Hitler simply confirmed them in their belief that appeasement was a feasible policy. From 1933 Lothian wrote and spoke in favour of Anglo-German friendship. In November 1933 he addressed a large and appreciative crowd at Nottingham, claiming amid applause that "in part, at any rate, that régime is the product of our own conduct in trying to exact impossible reparations and in requiring her [Germany] to be disarmed while her neighbours were armed to the teeth for fifteen years." No one in the meeting pointed out that Britain had successfully fought against the policy of "impossible reparations," and that these had been virtually abolished at Lausanne in 1932, before the régime they had "produced" had come to power. No one asked whether it was not perhaps reasonable that Germany's neighbours should hesitate to abandon their arms after a four years' war in which the Germans had invaded and held some of their territory. No one reminded the speaker that immediately after 1919 Britain had disarmed, conduct most unlikely to force Germany to adopt a militaristic attitude. But appeasement could flourish without argument. Its strength often lay in its apparent plausibility, not in its proven accuracy. Lothian's beliefs seemed unchangeable, despite the pressure of some of his friends; his visit to Hitler confirmed them. On his return he wrote in *The Times* that "Germany does not want war, and is prepared to renounce it absolutely as a method of settling her disputes with her neighbours." When his friend Abe Bailey, the South African mine owner, telegraphed, "Go slow. They purchased hundred thousand pounds commercial diamonds last month for military purposes," Lothian replied by sending him his *Times* articles and telling Bailey that Hitler had told him that Germany's one hope of being able to resist a Russian onslaught was friendship with Britain. To Lord Perth, the British Ambassador in Rome, who wondered whether Lothian might not have been deceived by Hitler's pleasant voice, Lothian replied:

> *Hitler is profoundly pre-occupied with Russia. He wants no quarrel with France and I do not think the National Socialists want to absorb the small Eastern European nations because that is contrary to their doctrine of race, though they* are *concerned with frontiers. . . .*
>
> *My own view is that Great Britain will get nowhere by joining up with the old encirclement group. That only means war. On the other hand, Germany does not want war.*

Lothian, like many advocates of appeasement in the Nazi area, did not base his opinions upon propaganda alone, nor was he entirely reliant upon his own interpretation of recent history. He sought sources that would enable him to make an independent judgement. In 1935 he made contact with Kurt Hahn, a refugee from Nazi persecution. As Private Secretary to Prince Max von Baden from 1917–20, Hahn had some inside knowledge of German policy-making. In England he had already founded Gordonstoun School on the model of the school he had founded at Salem in Germany, in 1920. In it, punishment, which could be severe, was regarded as expiation, and discipline thought to be maintained by creating a strong sense of guilt in every boy. Although Hahn was clearly a bona fide refugee from Nazism he was not entirely, in English terms, liberal-minded. Yet Lothian turned to him for guidance. Hahn responded by encouraging Lothian's hostility towards those who advocated the maintenance of the *status quo* established in 1919:

> *The makers and preservers of Versailles kept on denouncing Hitler but these, too, must be regarded as vested interests. I confess: to hear those who ought to be saying "Nostra culpa, nostra maxima culpa" exploiting the German situation to save themselves from a deservedly bad conscience, to listen to their boast: "We were right. We always told you so. That is the Bosche"—that makes me feel Nazi.*

Hahn was convinced that it was the refusal of the victors to grant Germany "equality" that made Nazism possible. And he felt certain that Nazism would continue to act irresponsibly for as long as Germany's neighbours failed to make some gesture of amity. In 1935 Churchill asked in public, as Lothian asked in private:

> *What manner of man is this grim figure who has performed these superb toils and loosed these frightful evils? Does he still share the passions he has evoked? Does he, in the full sunlight of worldly triumph, at the head of the great nation he has raised from the dust, still feel racked by the hatreds and antagonisms of his desperate struggle; or will they be discarded like the armour and cruel weapons of strife under the mellowing influences of success? Evidently a burning question for men of all nations!*

Churchill still hoped that the answer might not be an entirely foreboding one. He noted that those who had met Hitler found him "competent, cool, well-informed," and he concluded that "the world lives on hopes that the worst is over, and that we may yet live to see Hitler a gentler figure in a happier age." This was not a lone hope. Appeasement was rooted in the belief that human nature could not be entirely overwhelmed by evil, that even the most dangerous looking situation could be ameliorated, and that the most irascible politician could be placated, if treated with respect. As Kurt Hahn explained to Lothian, in words no doubt comforting to so staunch an advocate of appeasement:

> *Hitler has a warm, even a soft heart, which makes him over sensitive to suggestions that he is not hard enough. . . . The man feels he ought to keep his faith in his mission intact lest he should become "as sounding brass and tinkling cymbals." This is his mission: cure the hereditary curse of Germany—discord; sweep class war away; and make Germany respected again in the world, as an equal among equals. He does not want war, but he wants a peace in freedom, not a peace from impotence. . . . The peace of the world is not safe as long as Germany is surrounded by an atmosphere of distrust and revulsion.*

In Lothian's view even Nazi anti-semitism was not necessarily a permanent feature of Hitler's Germany. He felt that "in some degree the brutality of National Socialism is the reaction to the treatment given to Germany herself since the war," and could be assuaged if Germany were now given "her rightful place in Europe." Lothian reiterated these views as frequently as he could. He had many opportunities. His house at Blickling was a centre of social gatherings with political undertones. He wrote frequently to *The Times*. He spoke often at the Royal Institute of International

Affairs at Chatham House, where serious students of contemporary politics met and argued. He spoke in the House of Lords, and corresponded continuously with a widening circle of supporters and sceptics.

Lothian was not alone after 1933 in ascribing German extremism to British action, in supporting German rearmament, and in advocating Treaty revision in Germany's favour. Appeasement was a political philosophy which found adherents in all political parties and in all social classes. It was an attitude of mind common to many politicians, diplomats, civil servants, historians, journalists, industrialists, businessmen, shopkeepers, students, workers, and housewives. It was a policy of hope. Anyone who felt that war with Germany could be avoided, naturally tried to work out the best way of doing so. The most obvious means were conciliation and understanding. The idea, mooted by Churchill, of increasing British armaments until they were large enough to deter Hitler from war revived the belief that it was partly as a result of an "armaments race" that war had come in 1914. Believing a policy of rearmament to be an almost certain prelude to an inevitable clash of arms, people turned to the idea of discussions and concessions as being more likely to preserve peace. If Hitler could be persuaded that all his aims could be satisfied merely by his presenting them, and without the need for him even to threaten war, he would presumably opt automatically for peace.

Hitler's language was, at first glance, in no way conducive to appeasement. He constantly talked of resorting to force if he could not obtain satisfaction by other means. Yet in this very threat lay the strongest possible incentive to appeasement. Take Hitler at his word. To appease him, offer him satisfaction. Offer to help him in his search for Treaty revision, offer to accept German rearmament and the growing German Navy, illegal according to Versailles, offer to support his claim for the remilitarization of the Rhineland, offer to help him in his search for peaceful *Anschluss* with Austria and a peaceful rectification in Germany's favour of the Czech and Polish frontiers, offer to work out a means of giving Germany, if not a colony, certainly a share in the raw materials and resources of Africa. Appeasement had no shortage of suggestions. Often it was Hitler himself, not his British champions, who seemed to hesitate and hold back. Perhaps he could not believe that appeasement was a sincere policy; perhaps he felt that there would come a time when his demands would be challenged, and that too much show of friendship with Britain would make the British think that he was at bottom reliant upon British support. But he continued to see British visitors, and they continued to sing his praises and support his claims on their return to England.

As a public mood, appeasement flourished between 1933 and 1935; as a policy it languished. Foreign policy had to take into account a large number of problems, and relegated the Anglo-German problem to a secondary place. The war between Japan and China, and the war between Italy and Abyssinia, took up an increasing amount of time. Germany caused neither crises nor alarm on such a scale.

Appeasement suffered from another difficulty. In Government circles it failed to make an entirely favourable impression. Rumbold's successor as Ambassador in Berlin, Sir Eric Phipps, was as doubtful as Rumbold had been about the wisdom of accepting Germany's frequent official protestations of peaceful intent. Sir Warren Fisher, the Permanent Under-Secretary of State at the Treasury, considered that British efforts at rearmament were "ludicrously insubstantial." In 1935 he wrote to Baldwin about the proposed White Paper on rearmament, voicing the fears of many senior civil servants:

> *We are so convinced* (a) *of the reality of the danger of war,* (b) *of the profound ignorance of our own people,* (c) *of the degree to which they have been misled by so-called pacifist propaganda, that we feel that if any document is to serve a useful purpose it must be downright in its expression, and avoid all half-hearted or unconvincing phraseology. . . .*
>
> *It seems to me that the one thing of supreme importance is that our public should be warned in no uncertain language.*
>
> *I do therefore trust that the Cabinet may reconsider its attitude towards the purpose and form of the document, and address its mind not to gilding the pill for German consumption, but to ensuring that the pill provides the effective stimulation so much required by our sluggish-minded people.*

Although Baldwin was reluctant to commit himself to any strong challenge to Germany, and was being pressed by his friends to take more positive action in favour of appeasement, doubts as to the wisdom of too much compromise now permeated British policy-making. The Foreign Office, in particular, showed little enthusiasm from 1933–6 for Anglo-German rapprochement. If any one policy gained general approval it was that of appeasement with Italy, based on the hope of preventing Italy from drifting into the German orbit, and averting the danger of a hostile power in the Mediterranean that might threaten the Suez Canal, Britain's shortest link with the Indian Empire and Malaya. Vansittart was one of the officials most anxious for good relations between Britain and Italy. At the same time, he continued to warn against Germany. Although some politicians found his warnings verbose and repetitive, over-dramatized and over-ornate, they certainly influenced the Foreign Office, and made the appeasement of Germany seem a very risky, if not downright dangerous policy indeed.

Vansittart urged that "our rearmament is not proceeding fast enough or notoriously enough; and considerable doubt is being cast upon it abroad." Churchill, with whom Vansittart was in close contact, made this his theme in a series of parliamentary speeches. But the Government would not allow the doubts of a civil servant or the cries of a voice from the political wilderness to detract from what it still considered the practical and moral policy of European appeasement. Neville Chamberlain explained to his sister that in his opinion:

> *If we were now to follow Winston's advice and sacrifice our commerce to the manufacture of arms, we should inflict a certain injury on our trade from which it would take generations to recover, we should destroy the confidence which now happily exists, and we should cripple the revenue.*

On 21 June 1935 the public desire for appeasement received an official accolade. The British Government announced the conclusion of an Anglo-German Naval Agreement. This Agreement enabled Germany to build a navy up to a third of the size of the British Navy. It also authorized Germany to build, if she considered the circumstances warranted it, an equal number of submarines as Britain. This ended the naval restrictions imposed on Germany at

Versailles. As Germany was not a party to the Washington Naval Agreement, no limitation was imposed either—as was imposed on Britain—on the size or armaments of the ships she might build. In return for these major concessions, Hitler promised Britain that Germany would never use submarines against merchant shipping.

The Anglo-German Naval Agreement seemed a moral triumph for appeasement. It was also a political triumph for Baldwin, who succeeded MacDonald as Prime Minister two weeks before the Agreement was announced. It promised to inaugurate a period of positive appeasement. It seemed proof that Britain was determined, irrespective of the opinions of its former allies, to revise Versailles unilaterally, and to take Nazi Germany at its word. The Anglo-German Naval Agreement seemed an ideal form of appeasement. But was it as wise an agreement as the British Government claimed? Churchill was not alone in opposing it at the time, and a growing body of informed criticism grew up around it. Appeasement's most dramatic success, it was also a clear warning of danger if appeasement were pursued further on similar lines. The French, not having been consulted, were seriously offended. Mussolini, with whom we had agreed to consult about matters of mutual interest, saw Britain going cap-in-hand to Germany for bilateral compacts, and saw no reason why he should not now do likewise. The Russians, who, as a result of Barthou's prompting, were preparing the ground for a rapprochement with Britain, looked with alarm at an agreement whereby Britain seemed to hand over control of the seas in the Baltic to a German fleet. As a French diplomat remarked on hearing of the agreement, "It is not merely treachery, it is folly." Yet it appeared appeasement's finest hour. The Treaty of Versailles had been revised by the removal of clauses which even Lloyd George had considered imperative; and it had been revised without any concern for French interests or anxieties. It was based upon faith in Hitler's promise to accept an ultimate restriction on the number of ships he built, and in his pledge not to repeat Germany's Great War policy of sinking merchant shipping. If Hitler's promises were those of a rational statesman, in the Stresemann tradition, then the Agreement was clearly a triumph. Nor is there evidence that Baldwin, Neville Chamberlain, Anthony Eden, or Lord Halifax doubted Hitler's trustworthiness when the agreement was signed. They were all prominent members of the Government which had negotiated it. They all believed that it would prove effective. They all chose to ignore the growing signs of danger and deception.

Gustav Schmidt

The Domestic Background

In the following selection, Gustav Schmidt, professor of political science and international politics at the Ruhr University, Bochum, Germany, suggests that British attempts to pursue a strategy of "crisis avoidance" in the 1930s—a time of international depression and almost constant economic woes—were largely influenced by the desire of the National Governments of Baldwin and Chamberlain to avoid preoccupation with rearmament and, thus, endangerment of any hope of long-term economic recovery. The policy of acceptance of what were seen as legitimate German grievances—appeasement—was meant both to draw that nation away from a warlike agenda and, at the same time, allow British governments to devote resources to the social services demanded by their own electorate.

The role of domestic factors in British foreign policy has been examined on repeated occasions, albeit more within general terms of reference to the "no more war" atmosphere or the financial difficulties involved in introducing accelerated armament in time. Partly in view of its own negative historical experience, German research takes the British model of civil democracy as a premise for the theory that sound domestic policy is the most important prerequisite for the successful conduct of foreign affairs; accordingly pluralist systems—compared to dictatorships—are by no means

From "The Domestic Background to British Appeasement Policy," in Wolfgang J. Mommsen and Lothar Kettenacker, eds., *The Fascist Challenge and the Policy of Appeasement*, 1983, pp. 101–115. Harper Collins Ltd.

fighting a losing battle. British research, however, seems to be wary of seeing things in such euphemistic terms. In any case to underestimate domestic policy as a determining factor of foreign policy is to close one's eyes to important issues, for example, that the arms question had to be tackled *vis-à-vis* not only allies and enemies but also with regard to British public opinion. After all, expectations abroad diverged considerably from those of British interest groups. It is generally assumed on the basis of the French example that as "a direct impact of British domestic politics upon the foreign policy, the working of the democratic process" (in Great Britain and France) prejudiced adequate factual decision-making and was therefore a point of weakness. In view of the undisputed predominance of the Conservatives, corresponding in some respects to one-party rule in the 1930s, and the dominant position of Chamberlain in particular as Prime Minister and party leader in an "oligarchy of consensus," Donald Watt for example has reached the conclusion that "there was in Britain, in the formal sense, no direct interaction between British politics and British foreign policy in the years 1938/39." In application of this interpretation, the undeniable indulgence of British foreign policy towards the fascist powers must either be attributed to individuals and their weakness or the buck must be passed on to third parties—France, the opposition, the negligence of previous governments, and so on.

This conventional wisdom has recently been called into question in Britain by Cowling who illustrates that in its calculations British policy weighed up the danger in foreign policy just as much as the threat of socialism; for Cowling it is a question of how in an age of democracy the Conservatives could remain the dominant force in mass politics. Cowling has admittedly not drawn any conclusions from his views on the theme of "transformation of the class struggle by the challenge from Hitler"; his theory that Chamberlain's foreign policy and successful Conservative rule were interdependent remains an interesting topic for further research. It has therefore still to be explained how Chamberlain's confidence in the rationality of England's deterrent force as an element of appeasement could outlive the outbreak of war in 1939 despite the fact that the government was not determining the pace and extent of rearmament primarily by the dictates of foreign policy. In any case

Britain had not sought arrangements with her allies, such as staff talks with France, but pointed out that since Britain's defence programmes represented a vital insurance premium for her allies, it was her right to determine autonomously the extent and form of these security measures and to conduct exploratory talks with potential aggressors; by making use of contacts with Japan, Italy, and Germany it had been hoped that arms limitation could be achieved in certain sectors at least (naval, air force parity) and that the strain on British resources would thus be relieved. "The real hope for Europe," said Foreign Secretary Simon in 1935, is that "while the United Kingdom should make preparations as were necessary to defend herself, she should still pursue a policy of a settlement in which Germany could take an equal share."

Defence policy was to provide England with greater room to manoeuvre in foreign policy. As a result of the various domestic issues involved in the armament question, the importance of moments of crisis in foreign policy tended however to be played down within the continuous rearmament debate. Rearmament was not only considered from the point of view of whether and how one or other of the would-be partners could be assisted in the case of conflict but also with respect to how the external security dilemma would affect the development of the rearmament debate, demands on industry, and the position of social groups. At the time of the crisis in March 1936, for example, the French Ambassador in London, Corbin, observed quite correctly that the debate on the Defence White Paper—which was in fact the British "Four-Year Plan"—was being carried on as if the Rhineland had never been remilitarised. The defence debate was conducted primarily with regard to Britain's (narrowly defined) security interests; measures required were assessed with respect to their likely repercussions on the political stability and the industrial and financial "effective strength" of British society.

The government, however, hoped that the RAF—given priority—would act as a deterrent, in that it could lead to an encounter with the enemy around the negotiating table as opposed to on the battlefield. "I am pretty satisfied," wrote Chamberlain in 1936, "that, if only we can keep out of war a few years, we shall have an Air Force of such striking power that no one will care to run risks with it." This strategy was based on the assumption that Germany, although not necessarily Hitler himself, would gradually realise that it was not in a position to win the war since it had little with which to resist Britain's power of endurance (a united internal front, lines of communication with the USA and the dominions), its political strength.

My interpretation of British policy between the Depression and the Second World War is based on one particular overall impression: that the National Government, which over lengthy periods until just before the outbreak of war neither wanted, nor was in a position, to risk strategically stabilising measures of a military or economic nature at the trouble-spots in world politics, relied on the political strength of Great Britain as a justification and a safeguard for preventive diplomacy. Aware of both the deficiencies in defence accumulated during the Ten Years' Rule and changes in the world economic order which had restricted Britain's room for manoeuvre, the British government tended to regard political strength as a bastion from which it could demand a say in European affairs. The view that England contributed above all its economic and social stability to the balance of power implied that security policy was as anxious to preserve this source of strength as it was to account for the power shifts in the international scene by rearmament. Due to considerations relating to domestic politics, the USA was inconsistent in security policy; France's role as guardian of the Paris peace settlement of 1919–20 had been weakened by governmental crises and oscillations in economic policy. It therefore became all the more evident that a balance of inner stability had to be maintained: "Nothing operates more strongly," argued the Minister for the Co-ordination of Defence, Inskip, "to deter a potential aggressor from attacking this country than our stability . . . but were other countries to detect in us signs of strain, this deterrence would at once be lost."

Efforts to preserve political strength implied two prerequisites:

1. The safeguarding of relative autonomy in the government's political decision-making. This however meant that domestic decision-making processes had to be guarded against foreign interference wherever possible. Then and

only then would it be possible to react with flexibility in the case of crises provoked by Japan, Italy, or Germany.
2. If at all possible, those internal compromise settlements and agreements should be preserved which upheld Britain's position as an island of stability and common sense, free from the social unrest, civil war, and changes of regime on the Continent.

The first point implied guarding the existing social and economic order against revolutionary upheaval and excessive strain, the second "steering the course of modernisation and rejuvenation—the need for which in a period of rapid change and world-wide upheaval is also recognised by the conservative élite—along the path of evolution and under Conservative leadership."

British interest in safeguarding limited rearmament by means of a peaceful strategy was based on the assumption that if Britain were forced to rearm, setting off an inflationary spiral by excessive borrowing and a scramble for skilled labour and other scarce resources, the result would be a crisis similar to that of 1931. The policy of limited liabilities followed the principle of remaining for as long as possible below the threshold of the inflationary spiral which could be disastrous for the political and social system. The mobilisation of resources on behalf of security policy had to bear in mind that labour difficulties were probable as soon as defence measures developed their own dynamics in production. Despite growing concern about the "German peril" the perception of domestic dangers and risks determined the decision-making process in foreign and security policy and led the government alongside the application of the defence programme, considered as indispensable, to look for platforms for diplomatic action to keep the defence spiral in check and remove latent trouble-spots wherever possible. Appeasement policy was determined not so much by illusions on the Third Reich's willingness for negotiation and rapprochement but rather by fears of running into a domestic crisis triggered off by a rearmament race.

The overriding concern, repeatedly mentioned in the source materials, to avoid a recurrence of the crisis of 1931 does not define such a crisis as a revolutionary situation in itself but as the fear of being forced into a situation in which the existing political leadership might have to forfeit its democratic opportunity of being re-elected. The stabilisation of the system therefore required more than a mere Conservative class policy. It had to be made clear that the effects of security policy would not be one-sided and detrimental to the working class. By measures aimed at social appeasement and a continuing search for a European settlement the government tried to prevent losing face among its floating voters which could have resulted in the Conservatives being banished into political exile over a period of years. Following electoral defeat in 1929 Chamberlain, Baldwin, and other party leaders had reckoned with a long spell on the opposition benches. It was only the fall of the MacDonald minority government which had been tolerated by the Liberals that gave Baldwin, Chamberlain and Co. another opportunity of taking over the reins of government.

In view of the fact that Britain nevertheless finally declared war on the Third Reich in 1939 and in the decisive field of defence—the air force—caught up with and overtook Germany from 1939, it can be proved beyond doubt that the restraints of domestic policy produced no fatalism or resignation; limited rearmament was based on a careful weighing up of motives posed by both foreign and domestic policy, guided by British interests—the protection of national stability and the preservation of political strength, on the one hand, and on the other precautions for a buffer zone along the Rhine and in the Near East, disregarding *Mitteleuropa*.

Any interpretation of British appeasement must examine the criticism (put forward by Churchill in particular) that a government guided by a different "spirit" and led by "heroes" other than Baldwin, MacDonald, and Chamberlain could have stood up to the challenge from the Hitler regime and even prevented the outbreak of the Second World War. However, the persistence of appeasement policy in offering its services of mediation before and directly after Hitler's successful breakthroughs was backed up by the "no war" atmosphere within the country which expected policy to be aimed at preserving the peace rather than leading to mere "bloc formation and an arms race" as before 1914.

To protect Britain from further loss of substance the possibility of a working agreement had to be sounded out for as long as at all possible; this appeared necessary not only due to the weakness of France but in particular to the view that the onus of any action in resisting Germany's "Griff nach der Weltmacht" [grab for world power] would be on Britain, just as in the First World War. Since Britain would therefore be dependent on her own resources it seemed justifiable for London to examine—if necessary single-handedly—the possibilities of containing the damage threatened or already caused by Germany. British foreign policy claimed a leading role in correcting the course of events since 1919 to clear the atmosphere, but (up to 1938) declined, because of "over-commitments," the responsibility implied by great power status, for example, to make gestures or grant economic assistance to smaller nations, encouraging them to stand up to the dictatorships. The problem was who would bear the burden of adjustment between "satisfied" nations and "have-nots"; as the question had arisen time and time again since 1918–19, government departments in the 1930s concluded from their search for an agreement that there was only one way out: the inevitable sacrifices implied in a general European settlement would have to be made by third powers. The Foreign Office put forward—but to no avail—that Britain should be prepared to pay for concessions out of her own pocket by experimenting with colonial appeasement; this, however, came up against the brick wall of a lobby largely opposed to changing the measures implemented in 1931–2, but in favour of political appeasement (that is, conceding Central Europe as a zone of German influence).

Confident of its political strength—also respected by Germany—and of its own negotiating skill, British diplomacy ran the risk of Germany questioning the *status quo* in exploratory talks; still, it was hoped that the essentials of the Western powers could be discussed in a way that change in the *status quo* and German concessions could be tied together as part and parcel of a comprehensive settlement. However, attempts to transform crises into a comprehensive settlement by means of preventive diplomacy—that is, appeasement offensives—were condemned by German policy as "diplomacy of illusion."

The economic departments—the Treasury, the Board of Trade, the Ministry of Agriculture, the Ministry of Labour—contested the leading role of the Foreign Office in decision-making on foreign policy. They claimed their due share of responsibility in the light of the economic, financial, and social burdens occasioned by the security policy *vis-à-vis* the dictators now that the other pillars of international society, that is, France and the United States, had withdrawn their support. It was not in fact the department formally in charge of foreign relations that determined action necessary to safeguard Britain's security interests at international trouble-spots, but the Treasury, insisting that Britain's commitments be defined in terms of her economic possibilities. The Treasury enforced the principle that the Cabinet should ensure that foreign policy priorities remained in harmony with defence burdens; it argued that the supplies required for a continental commitment would not only overtax the economy but, compared to what the air force and the navy could offer by way of defence for Britain, would constitute misguided investment; the Foreign Office was thus deprived of its pledge of a "common fate" with France which, in collaboration with French politicians, it tried to impose on British policy. The requirements of the army, the Cinderella of the defence forces, were repeatedly disregarded: to meet them could have led to a dislocation of industries without providing a sufficient safeguard for British security. Chamberlain and Runciman applied the principle that demands on industry and not demands advocated by the service departments and the Foreign Office should be taken as a yardstick for the armament process which actually only began in 1936. For to decide that the production capacities required in the event of a war should be prepared and utilised even before the potential conflict, would be to subject trade and industry to damage from which it could only expect to recover after generations—if at all. The economic departments, industrial advisers, and leading economic circles gained acceptance for their opinion that accelerated rearmament would destroy the confidence which guaranteed the basis for economic revival and an increase of national revenue.

Those in Cabinet responsible for economic policy were unwilling to undo the package of measures introduced (1931-3) to guard the British economy from the adverse effects of international economic events for the sake of Britain's alliance policy. The more difficult it became to conduct "business as usual," while at the same time building up peacetime strength to the required level of the programmes, the more rigorously they defended their point of view.

Interest in avoiding a deterioration of relations with labour also spoke for caution in security policy. The government was convinced that Britain could put up with risks in foreign policy more easily than a conflict with labour. Therefore the argument that defence programmes could only be implemented if labour co-operated played a prominent role in discussion at Cabinet level. The government's assurances that rearmament should for as long as possible be organised on the basis of the willing co-operation of industry and the unions ran along the same lines. Accordingly it would have been appropriate to have conducted top-level talks, not only with the FBI [Federation of British Industries] but also with the unions—and before the spring of 1938. In the first talks in the autumn of 1935, however, it had become clear that as a result of the close organisational links between the trade union movement and the Labour Party, the relations between the government and the TUC [Trades Union Congress] were of a different nature to those between the government and industrial umbrella organisations. The government—emphatically advised by the unions (Bevin) that it should address its efforts to the Labour Party—was neither willing nor in a position to play off the unions against the party; neither did it yield—after Munich—to the temptation of depriving the Labour Party of the fruits of its publicity campaign (to an even greater extent than by the November 1935 elections)—for this would only result in bitterness and jeopardise industrial co-operation in the foreseeable future. However, these considerations did not go so far as to lead the government to consult either labour or the Labour Party. A number of arguments were raised in Cabinet against such consultations: such an invitation would signal an emergency situation and in view of the international situation would put public opinion into a state of alarm; the majority tended to repudiate any threat of war. If it were to come to official negotiations on support for economic and industrial mobilisation, that is, labour's consent to dilution, and so on, then it would have to be expected that labour would make demands in return—not only on foreign policy (the incorporation of the Soviet Union into active peace policy, consultation with the League of Nations on the Sudetenland question), but also on economic and social policy (conscription of wealth, paid holidays, compensatory wage increases, and so on). It is not improbable that the government wanted to wait for events in Europe to teach labour a lesson—in other words, it was hoped that faced with external pressure the "sectional prejudices" against intervention into so-called union practices would gradually subside, so that the government would neither have to make political compromises nor be forced to demand sacrifices from the employers (excess duty with regard to profiteering, wealth tax) similar to the sacrifices expected from labour (transfer of labour forces into the armament industry). The National Defence Contribution, the only large-scale attempt to impose a substantial and symbolic burden on business, had been a disaster for Chamberlain. Although Chamberlain was aware of the need not only to distribute sacrifices evenly but also to consult labour representatives on arrangements in the event of a war, governmental policy was not in a position to create such a balance.

This can be partly explained by the Cabinet's inability to pursue a clear-cut line in security and defence policy: agreement on the guidelines of defence policy was, however, a prerequisite for consultation with the opposition—otherwise their leaders would outline their own terms of reference, thus prejudicing governmental policy.

The need for a foreign and defence policy *geared towards public opinion*—conjuring up images of prewar diplomacy and the crisis of July 1914 as a deterrent—could be used by Britain in critical phases of negotiation as a standard argument—in particular *vis-à-vis* France—for excluding "irrevocable decisions at this stage" and remaining open instead to possible developments in the German camp; moreover, for concrete reasons (by-elections, the peace ballot campaign, the Hoare-Laval débâcle, opposition to the Unemployment Assistance Board Act) it was even more imperative to take the domestic background to decision-making into consideration. Furthermore, it became obvious that the scope of Britain's partner, France, was also subject to such constraints. British preventive diplomacy, aware of the symptoms of crisis in French politics, in particular the disparity between Paris and the French people (the provincial press), was confirmed in its own claim to leadership *vis-à-vis* its wavering ally; given the discredited French line it demanded the support of *public* opinion in both countries for the British strategy. British politicians moreover had the impression "that the country will not allow us to take drastic action in what they regard as a pure French interest." The response to German action on 16 March 1935 for instance, without prior consultation with France and Italy was justified by Foreign Secretary Simon who said that the government would have had to put forward and carry out a "British policy"; had London delayed the announcement until an allied memorandum of protest had been drawn up, "British opinion would have gone against France."

This regard for public opinion finally meant that the decision-making process was partly blocked; the government and public opinion convinced themselves that basically Germany's demands for revision were justified and that both the means of enforcement and the moral justification for even limited measures of retaliation were lacking. Influenced by feelings of guilt about Britain's share of responsibility for Versailles and convinced that an Anglo-German conflict had to be avoided, flexibility was called for in British policy on questions which were classified as "local" German demands—the range of which was extended from equality of status (in armament) via the Rhineland to the annexation of Austria. Since even the anti-appeasers approved overtures to Germany—"The approach would have been worth taking (even if Germany declined the terms offered) as putting us right with our own public opinion"—the real problem was practically ignored, that is, the extent to which England's desire for peace and corresponding willingness to negotiate would tip the balance of power in favour of the Third Reich. Potentially dangerous developments which both the government and public opinion had played down (internally) could not suddenly be put forward as a matter of life and death in the event of a critical turn of the tide in Europe. This situation was exacerbated by the fact that the government, in order to keep domestic repercussions at a minimum, tried to dissociate debates on defence programmes from discussions on concrete commitments in foreign policy; moreover, the March crises provoked by the Third Reich just happened to take place while government and opposition were busy defining their positions for the budgetary debates on defence estimates and at a time when at the annual meetings of the constituency parties they could sound reaction at grass-root level. Reports on the general atmosphere reinforced the view that the government would only find support for defence policy if the dip into the taxpayer's pocket were accompanied by an announcement of continued endeavours to strike a balance with Germany and in particular an agreement on arms limitation. "The policy . . . seemed rather to be that some diplomatic approach to Germany would greatly assist in the preparation of the Defence Programme next month."

Decision-makers were in agreement on their assessment of public opinion as crises came to a head. The steps taken by Germany were to have been expected and understandable in substance if not in form. The crises should not be used as justification for even more specific defence programmes. Since it had been stressed that it was necessary to replace the obsolete provisions of the Treaty of Versailles by realistic regulations with the aid of legalised German rearmament, British rearmament could not solely be justified as a reaction to the German peril, at least not without associating German armament with the dangers emanating from a dictatorship. If however a tactic were adopted whereby the threat of an attack from Germany was dangled in front of the public's eyes without events actually justifying such a warning (this did not happen until Prague), then all motives and interests aimed at limited armament would have to be thrown overboard. To summarise: it can be said that appeasement as a strategy of crisis avoidance was largely coloured not only by the traditions of British political culture but by domestic circumstances.

Simon, Chancellor of the Exchequer (and former Foreign Secretary), for example, argued against out and out adjustment to National Socialist Germany's rearmament policy; in his opinion to implement such programmes would transform British society and politics beyond all recognition; unlike the German rulers Britain neither wanted nor was in a position to neglect the social security system or write off the foreign debt with the mere stroke of a pen.

In a similar vein, Eden, in a statement to foreign press correspondents, justified persistent efforts towards appeasement with the argument that Britain should not seek confrontation in foreign policy—the government's entire domestic policy was aimed at avoiding confrontation; bloc formation and the doctrine of class struggle were a threat to peace at home and abroad alike. Reflecting the basic conviction of British Conservatives, Premier Baldwin and Foreign Secretary Eden declared that it was preferable to repair a leaking dam—that is, to reconstruct it on a line of retreat—rather than to charge against the floods on an advance front. Instead of sabre-rattling and manoeuvring into a situation where swords would have to be drawn, it was necessary, precisely in times of crisis, to show willingness to negotiate and at the same time to make it clear which operative ideals would under no circumstances be called into question. By acting in a businesslike manner and showing or feigning indifference to positions based on different forms of ideology, a working agreement was to be induced giving no special advantage to either side. Until the opposite had been proved—that is, dictatorial/Bonapartist action in foreign policy—there seemed to be no reason why a political culture in which peaceful change was seen as the essence of a class society (in the guise of the deferrent system) and of the empire/commonwealth should not also try out this domestic approach in the field of foreign affairs. As regards the question of whether normal relations with the Third Reich were possible (a peaceful revision of the *status quo*), confidence was placed in the soothing effect of the strategy of crisis tried out in domestic policy: by making concessions on demands for a change of the *status quo* considered as legitimate grievances, the integrity of the overall system was to be upheld. The ventures into the fields of economic and political appeasement had this aim in mind. Aware of the fact that the German war economy was bound to accelerate German withdrawal from the world economic order (a trend begun with barter trade and foreign exchange control) and threaten the very existence of that system, British policy aimed at reinforcing the position of the "moderates" and keeping Germany within the Western capitalist system. Nevertheless, in the course of the 1930s British policy had less and less success in drawing the line between adjustment to shifts in the balance of power and interests which would maintain the system on the one hand, and on the other endangering the whole system by giving up objectives which in the past had served as evidence of solidarity and common security interests.

Whereas, British domestic policy, precisely on account of its limited approach to the armament question, signalled its interest in a stabilisation of the system, foreign policy took a critical turn, since one of the parties involved—Hitler—used British reticence to revolutionise the balance of power, while the scope of the other protagonist—France—remained limited. The fact that appeasement as moulded by British domestic politics was conceived as a counter-offensive to the *Machtpolitik* of the National Socialist system (and to the—previous—*status quo* diplomacy of France) faced totally different circumstances and adversaries in the domestic and foreign fields, explains the discrepancy between the relative success of the internal immunisation strategy and the fatal consequences of the "as if" policy in foreign affairs.

Michael Howard

British Military Preparations

Michael Howard, formerly Regis Professor of Modern History at Oxford and now professor of history at Yale University, examines the problems faced by British military planners in the appeasement period. They were influenced by three major factors: the need to protect a world empire, the new vulnerability to air attack of the home islands that had for many centuries been immune to seaborne invasion, and, finally, the undeniable fact that resources for military spending were limited by economic conditions and the reluctance of the government to endanger recovery through lavish military budgets. As Professor Howard illustrates, the international situation ultimately demanded of military and political leaders a policy both of rearmament and, finally, of war, even though not one of these three difficulties was resolved.

From "British Military Preparations for the Second World War," in David Dilks, ed., *Retreat from Power: Studies in Britain's Foreign Policy in the Twentieth Century*, 1981, pp. 102–107. Reprinted by permission of the author.

In tracing the sad, confusing and nearly disastrous history of British attempts to come to terms with the realities of power politics in the 1930s, it is useful to bear in mind the three major factors which determined British defence policy between the wars.

British Defence Policy was, in the first place, concerned with the protection of an empire; of what we would today call "a global system." British defence planners had to provide not simply for the security of the United Kingdom, but for that of such countries as Egypt, India, the Federated Malay States, Australia, New Zealand and a host of minor colonial possessions. The foundation of this Imperial system was, in the 1930s, as it had been in the 1890s, the Royal Navy's capacity to maintain "command of the sea," in order to safeguard Imperial communications. In 1896 the Admiralty had laid it down in words which were to be repeatedly quoted in official documents:

> *The maintenance of sea supremacy has been assumed as the basis of the system of Imperial defence against attack from over the sea. This is the determining factor in shaping the whole defensive policy of the Empire, and is fully recognised by the Admiralty who have accepted the responsibility of protecting all British territory against organised invasion from the sea.*

All British territory: this was a heavy responsibility, and one which grew heavier as the 1930s pursued their increasingly depressing course. In 1932 when it was clear that the Japanese were pursuing a "forward policy" on the mainland of China which it was feared might lead to an equally forward policy elsewhere in the Pacific, the Australian government made anxious enquiries in London as to whether the Royal Navy still felt itself capable of fulfilling those responsibilities. They received from the British Chiefs of Staff the following answer:

> *Provided that the British fleet arrives in time and finds a properly equipped base at Singapore, Australia has nothing to fear beyond a sporadic attack.*

But if the Fleet did *not* arrive in time, and if it did not find a properly equipped base at Singapore, then, it was clearly implied, Australian interests and even territory become exposed to attack on a considerable scale. And not only Australia would be at risk: New

Zealand, Malaya, Burma, India, the Persian Gulf, the British possessions on the east coast of Africa, in short the whole of the Indian Ocean would be vulnerable to Japanese naval attack. So throughout the 1930s the eyes of the Admiralty were fixed on what appeared to them to be the greatest threat to the British imperial system: the navy of Japan, second in size only to that of the British and the United States. We have to bear this in mind if we are to understand the reluctance of successive First Sea Lords and First Lords of the Admiralty to see the Navy saddled with additional responsibilities in Europe and in the Mediterranean, especially at the time of the Italo-Abyssinian war.

The Chiefs of Staff in the 1930s were not a particularly memorable group, but by far the most impressive among them was the First Sea Lord between 1932 and 1938, Admiral Sir Ernle Chatfield, Chairman of the Chiefs of Staff Committee. Chatfield was one of those primarily responsible for the conclusion of the Anglo-German naval agreement of 1935, whereby the Germans agreed not to build more than thirty-five per cent of the British strength in all classes of vessel, with the remarkable exception of submarines; a self-denying ordinance which in the existing state of the German economy and rearmament imposed no sacrifices on Nazi Germany but which left the Royal Navy (or so it was hoped) free to fulfil its commitments in the Far East. Chatfield, moreover, was particularly insistent at the time of the Italo-Abyssinian crisis in 1935 that Britain should not become involved in a conflict in the Mediterranean; not because the Royal Navy doubted its ability to defeat the Italian navy, but because in the process of doing so it might incur losses which would make it all the more difficult to get an effective fleet to Singapore if a crisis developed in the Far East. In the eyes of the Royal Navy, the Far East enjoyed overriding priority almost until the end of the decade.

The Army also saw its duties primarily in terms of Imperial defence. The garrisoning and the protection of India, Burma, the Middle Eastern countries and the colonies in Africa had been the main and continuing concern of the British Army ever since those regions had come under British suzerainty. It was an *actual* commitment to which the Army had to give a standing priority in terms of training and equipment, over a *hypothetical* involvement in a

Continental war which there was a profound reluctance on the part of the entire country, including the Army itself, to contemplate at all. A skeleton "Expeditionary Force" existed on paper, but when in 1925 the British government assumed certain specific obligations to continental intervention under the terms of the Treaty of Locarno, the Chiefs of Staff warned the Cabinet that although

> *the Expeditionary Force, together with a limited number of Air Force squadrons, constitute the only military instrument for immediate use in Europe or elsewhere outside Imperial territory in support of foreign policy, they are so available only when the requirements of Imperial defence so permit. It follows that so far as commitments on the Continent are concerned, the services can only take note of them.*

It is hard to conceive of a more alarming disjunction between foreign and defence policy than that expressed in this statement.

Imperial Defence thus enjoyed absolute priority in the plans both of the Royal Navy and of the Army, and European obligations received only such crumbs as could be spared from that table. This situation was gradually to be modified in the course of the 1930s, but it was not wholly transformed until the very eve of the Second World War.

The second factor was the vulnerability of the United Kingdom to air attack. It was to deal with this problem that an independent Royal Air Force had been reconstituted after the First World War. If the Admiralty accepted as its responsibility the defence of imperial territory and communications, the Royal Air Force existed in order to prevent an air attack on the United Kingdom from a European adversary. But it was assumed until about 1937, for good technical reasons, that effective defence against aerial attack was not feasible. There could be no physical defence; there could only be deterrence. So it was the function of the Royal Air Force to provide a *deterrent* against any conceivable attack on the United Kingdom, by possessing the capacity to inflict unacceptable and unavoidable punishment against the homeland of any aggressor. The concept of "deterrence" with which we have become only too familiar since the Second World War was in fact developed by the British Air Staff in the 1920s in a very sophisticated form. The vulnerability to air bombardment of Britain in general, and of London in particular, increasingly haunted the British government and British public opinion between the wars. A subcommittee of the Committee of Imperial Defence in 1921 drew a gruesome picture of what could happen in the event of air attack. "Railroad traffic would be disorganised, food supplies interrupted, and it is probable that after being subjected for several weeks to the strain of such an attack, the population would be so demoralised that they would insist on an armistice."

This forecast was based on an assumed attack from France by an Air Force capable of dropping only seventy-five tons of bombs a day. But by 1939 planners were expecting raids on a scale of 700 tons a day; coming not from France, against whom retaliation was comparatively simple, but from a Germany whose own civilian targets were too dispersed and too distant for an effective return strike to be at that time feasible. Not only did they foresee a daily strike of 700 tons; they also warned of the possibility of an immediate "knock-out blow" against London of 3500 tons, inflicting some fifty casualties per ton of bombs. In fact the heaviest load dropped on the United Kingdom during the war was to be 1000 tons dropped in a raid on London in April 1941; the next heaviest, the 500 tons dropped on Coventry in November of 1940. Otherwise the general average of raids fluctuated between about 40 tons and 300 tons.

Clearly the prime responsibility of the Government was to protect the people of the United Kingdom, which obviously involved a high priority for expenditure on the Royal Air Force. But it also involved an additional responsibility for the Army. In any case the Army was responsible for anti-aircraft defences; but in addition it would have the task of maintaining order in a civil community whose reaction under this kind of bombardment was unpredictable, and might well be one of uncontrollable panic. So in 1938 the air defence of Great Britain was accepted as the Army's main responsibility, one even more urgent than that of imperial defence.

The third factor in planning was, simply, money. Much has been made by hostile critics of the unwillingness of British governments in the 1930s to spend enough on rearmament, or to interfere with the normal course of trade. It is easy and perhaps legitimate to condemn the Treasury officials who advised them for a certain narrow-minded conservatism, for ignoring the words of wisdom, laced plentifully with acid, which dropped from the lips of Maynard Keynes, for the caution imposed on them by the disastrous experiences of 1929 to 1931, in short for their conviction that the convalescent economy of the United Kingdom was simply not in a state to support the heavy additional charges required by rearmament on the scale which the Chiefs of Staff demanded. When it was suggested in 1934 that a defence loan might be raised to meet some of the costs of rearmament, Neville Chamberlain, Chancellor of the Exchequer, described this as "the broad road that leads to destruction." The idea of raising the standard rate of income tax to something above five shillings (25p) in the pound was regarded as almost inconceivable in the financial climate of the 1930s. Yet the problem which faced the government was not simply that of redistributing resources from the civilian into the military sector, of reallocating priorities. It was the more basic one of enabling the country to go on earning its living during this period. The Permanent Under-Secretary to the Treasury, Sir Warren Fisher, defined the problem in 1934 as follows:

> *Raw materials, not to mention food, are only produced within this country in relatively negligible quantities, and therefore have to be secured from other countries who will not of course give us them. And when our international purchasing power is exhausted they will not continue indefinite credit to us.*

So even if the British government committed all its resources to rearmament and defence, it would still have to trade abroad in order to purchase the necessary raw materials and food for its civilian population and its armies. It had considerable overseas assets but not enough to make possible an unfavourable balance of payments for the indefinite future.

This was the nightmare which stalked the corridors of the Treasury in the 1930s, and when war finally came, the nightmare came true. Early in 1940, the Treasury reported that by the end of that year the United Kingdom's overseas liabilities would total some £400 million. The assets in gold reserves and marketable securities were only £700 million; Britain would be bankrupt by the end of 1941 even if the rate of spending did not increase; which in fact it did. It is easy now to forget that in the 1930s there was no reason to assume that the United States would bail the United Kingdom out of any war in which she became involved. In fact Congress, by a succession of Neutrality Acts, was making it clear that she would do nothing of the kind. The British empire was alone, with such Continental allies as it might be able to recruit. There was no exaggeration in the statement which Sir Thomas Inskip, the Minister for the Co-ordination of Defence, made to the Cabinet in February 1938:

> *the plain fact which cannot be obscured is that it is beyond the resources of this country to make proper provision in peace for the defence of the British Empire against three major powers in three different theatres of war.*

. . . [In 1936, when serious rearmament finally began,] heavy weight was still placed on the air deterrent, and Chamberlain and his colleagues continued to resist the creation of a British Expeditionary Force. In the summer of 1937 Chamberlain became Prime Minister and shelved the proposal by setting up a new enquiry under the new Minister for Co-ordination of Defence, Sir Thomas Inskip, whose task was to advise how British defence commitments could be brought in line with her financial capacity.

The abolition of the BEF was not entirely the result of Chamberlain's insistence. Outside events played into his hands. In the Mediterranean the explosion of Italian power put Egypt under direct threat for the first time. Simultaneously, there was the outbreak of civil disturbance in Palestine which began in 1936, and continued at an intensity which ultimately absorbed eighteen battalions of the British Army; disorders on the scale of those in Northern Ireland today, and only less serious in that they were rather further away. Further, the disturbance in Palestine affected all the Muslim countries in the Middle East, where Britain was with increasing difficulty trying to preserve her precarious suzerainty; which involved further "peacekeeping" obligations for the Army in Egypt and Iraq. Finally the growing anticipated weight of the German air attack on the United Kingdom made it appear necessary to divert increasing military resources to the Air Defence of Great Britain. This did not leave much for an Expeditionary Force for the Continent. By February 1938 it had shrunk to two infantry divisions and one mobile division, lightly equipped "for an eastern theatre." It was to be available for Continental commitments, in the words of the Secretary of State for War, Mr. Leslie Hore-Belisha,

> *only if the situation in the rest of the world permits, and it would be necessary for the General Staff to review the whole field of possible action open to the enemy before this could be determined.*

Once more we see how the primacy of Imperial defence, combined with the constraints imposed by limited resources, eliminated the option of making a military contribution in Europe. This was the position in March 1938 when the *Anschluss* between Germany and Austria pointed to the possibility, in the very near future, of a German attack on Czechoslovakia. Immediately after the *Anschluss* the Chiefs of Staff were asked to report on the military situation which would result from such an attack. In the course of their review they gave the following warning:

> *No pressure that we and our possible allies can bring to bear, either by sea, on land, or in the air, could prevent Germany from invading and over-running Bohemia and from inflicting a decisive defeat on the Czechoslovakian army. We should then be faced with the necessity of undertaking a war against Germany for the purpose of restoring Czechoslovakia's lost integrity and this object would only be achieved by the defeat of Germany and as the outcome of a prolonged struggle. In the world situation today it seems to us that if such a struggle were to take place, it is more than probable that both Italy and Japan would seize the opportunity to further their own ends, and that in consequence the problem we have to envisage is not that of a limited European war only, but of a world war.*

This would be the war against the three adversaries which at all costs had to be avoided. As for the balance of terror in the air, it was estimated in autumn 1938 that Germany had some 5000 first line aircraft against the British 1500, while the French did not have any aircraft capable of bombing Germany at all. So if Germany were to concentrate on a "knock-out blow" against England—a possibility which could not be discounted—she would be able to deliver the tonnage of high explosive described above: 500–600 tons a day for two months. Since the Royal Air Force could only retaliate with 100 tons a day for a far shorter time, measurable at most in weeks and possibly in days, and since Germany presented no comparable targets, the Air Staff advised that it would be unwise to initiate air attack upon industrial targets in Germany; it would be "inadequate to produce decisive results and must inevitably provoke immediate reprisal action on the part of Germany, at a time when our defence measures at home, both active and passive, are very far from complete."

Such was the advice given by the Chiefs of Staff to the British government of the day. It was advice that Chamberlain could not ignore, even if it was not the primary factor in his decision, in September 1938, to conclude the Munich agreement with Hitler at the expense of the Czechs. Certainly that agreement was greeted by the Chiefs of Staff with profound relief. It gave them time to press on with their defences, above all with the Air Defence of Great Britain which was now giving them some hope of being able to counter the threat of German air bombardment.

The Chiefs of Staff has always reckoned that by 1939 they might just be in a position to undertake a serious war against Germany. And since 1937, developments had been taking place in the field of aerial technology and radar, which was for the first time making defence against air attack a feasible proposition. But it was going to take another two years before fighter aircraft of adequate performance, Hurricanes and Spitfires, and radio-location stations in sufficient quantity could be installed and in working order. But the surrender at Munich had one unforeseen result. It had to be accepted that as a result of the cession of the Sudeten areas, Czechoslovakia would be virtually defenceless. What had not been foreseen was the effect which this would have on French morale. In December 1938, reports began to reach the Cabinet from the British embassy and the British Military Attaché in Paris, about the fundamental reappraisal which was taking place in Paris about the whole direction of French policy. France no longer had the ally in the East on whom she had been relying to tie down a substantial proportion of the German Army. She looked with increasing alarm at the growing imbalance, not simply of military strength, but of male population between Germany and France. And there seemed to the British officials to be a distinct danger that France in the near future might reorientate her policy completely and line up with Germany if the British did not do something drastic and dramatic to prevent it. What the French wanted from Britain was, in the gruesome words of the British Military Attaché, *un éffort du sang*: an effort of blood. They wanted, in short, British troops. It would not be enough for Frenchmen to be told that the Royal Navy was commanding the seas from the Mediterranean to Singapore, or that the Royal Air Force was knocking all hell out of Düsseldorf while the Germany army was trampling through the fields of Picardy and massacring Frenchmen by hundreds of thousands as they had done between 1914 and 1917. As the Chiefs of Staff admitted in a report to the Cabinet in February 1939,

> *it is difficult to say how the security of the United Kingdom could be maintained if France were forced to capitulate and therefore defence of the former may have to include a share in the land defence of French territory.*

So in February 1939 the Cabinet agreed to throw financial caution to the winds and create not simply an expeditionary force of six divisions, but a full-scale Continental army of thirty-two divisions. But it was a little late in the day to do this. There were no training facilities and above all no armament. If sometimes one wonders why the British Army did not perform better in the first three years of the war, the short answer is that it only came into existence as a force organised for Continental warfare in the early spring of 1939.

The decision to create a Continental army, and to enter into staff conversations with the French, was taken even before Hitler overran the rest of Czechoslovakia on 14 March 1939. This event, however, set on foot a very belated search for allies in Eastern Europe, including the Soviet Union, in order to re-constitute an eastern front, to deny the economic resources of south-east Europe to Germany, and to create a protective glacis to the north of Britain's position in the East Mediterranean.

And what of the Mediterranean? The Chiefs of Staff assumed that Italy would enter the war on the side of the Germans. They therefore favoured the creation of an alliance in the Balkans consisting of Greece, Yugoslavia, and Turkey, to hold her in check. But those powers could only provide, and be provided with, help if the Royal Navy commanded the Mediterranean; and that, also, would be the necessary condition if the restive Muslim world in the Middle East was to be kept under control. Yet the first priority of the Royal Navy was to hold a fleet in readiness to go to the relief of Singapore. What would happen in the Pacific if Japan took the offensive?

In the summer of 1939, in a series of anguished papers, the Admiralty wrestled with this problem. They simply did not have enough ships to go round. It had always been assumed, and the Australians in particular had always been assured, that the Far East would enjoy an absolute priority over the Mediterranean. Now the situation was transformed. The Admiralty could only report in June 1939 that

> *there are so many variable factors which cannot at present be assessed, that it is not possible to state definitely how soon after Japanese intervention a fleet could be despatched to the Far East; neither is it possible to enumerate precisely the size of the fleet that we could afford to send.*

This was the situation when war broke out in September 1939. Of the three problems which I listed at the beginning of this paper as dominating British defence policy, not one had been solved. In the field of Imperial defence, Britain was no longer in a position to ensure the defence of her eastern empire. In economic terms she was within two years of total bankruptcy. Only in the defence of Britain against air attack had progress been made. Such defence was at last becoming feasible, in spite of the dogma on which all RAF strategic thinking had rested, that any such development was out of the question. What however was certainly not feasible was the kind of "deterrent" air attacks against Germany which the Royal Air Force had believed to be the only way of defending the population of the United Kingdom.

Nevertheless in April 1939 the British Chiefs of Staff produced in discussion with their French colleagues a realistic plan for winning the forthcoming war, which was to become the basis of Anglo-French strategy, and later of Anglo-American strategy. This saw the war as consisting of three phases. In the first, nothing could be done except hold the line against a German attack which was bound to be ferocious but could only be short-lived. If that could be survived, then there was some hope. In the second phase, the Allies should contain Germany while dealing decisively with Germany's expected associate, Italy; and the elimination of Italy would be facilitated if Italian morale had been undermined by the capture of Italian possessions in North and East Africa. During this phase the allied bomber effort should be directed against economic and industrial objectives in Germany with the object of contributing to the ultimate breakdown of her resistance. Third, "the final object of the Allies is to defeat Germany. In view of the magnitude of the reserves which would have to be employed no date and no possible line of action can be fixed for this phase. But meanwhile," concluded the plan, "in peace, as later in war, all the resources of diplomacy should be devoted to securing the benevolent neutrality or active assistance of other powers, particularly the United States of America."

This was what British military planners were intending to do in April 1939. It is consoling to observe that this was precisely what Britain and her allies ultimately did. It would be too much to claim for the planners of 1939 a substantial share of the credit for winning the war. But it was certainly due in some degree to their sensible and far-sighted provisions that the war was not quickly and irretrievably lost.

September 1936: A characteristic pose by the Fuhrer, addressing the Nazi faithful at the Nuremberg Party Rally. (UPI/Bettmann)

PART

III The Crises

Telford Taylor

The Abyssinian Crisis

Since mid-1934 it was becoming clear that Benito Mussolini meant to attack Abyssinia, modern Ethiopia, to add to his "new Roman Empire" and avenge the Italian defeat at Adowa in 1896. In the hope of heading off the open warfare that would put collective security to the test, Sir Samuel Hoare (who became foreign secretary in mid-1935) pursued a "double policy" of bluff against aggression coupled with overtures of compromise toward Italy. Telford Taylor, jurist and historian as well as former senior American prosecutor at the Nuremberg War Crimes Trials, discusses not only the impossible position caused by this policy but also the other influences that brought the government of Stanley Baldwin to attempt so foolhardy a gambit as the Hoare-Laval agreement of December 1935.

Baldwin and the other ministers failed to foresee the contradictions into which Hoare's policy was leading them, and continued through July and early August to pin their hopes on "a fair settlement within the League." To this end, in mid-August Eden and Vansittart (Hoare being temporarily disabled by arthritis) went to Paris for discussions with Laval and the Italian Ambassador, Vittorio Cerruti. Various compromise proposals were put to the Italians, but Mussolini rejected them all and demanded extensive annexation and an Italian mandate from the League over the entire country. This was far more than the British could stomach, and Eden left Paris convinced that a crisis was inevitable and that the French would be of little help in its resolution. Baldwin returned from vacationing in France for an emergency meeting of the Cabinet on August 22 and authorized the Admiralty to make such disposition of the Navy as was necessary to meet the possibility of war with Italy.

The Chief of the Naval Staff, Admiral Ernle Chatfield, at once moved the Mediterranean fleet from Malta to Alexandria, so as to lessen the danger of an Italian air attack. He had no doubt that the Navy was strong enough to deal with the Italians, but warned the ministers that it would sustain losses—perhaps as high as four battleships—which would seriously weaken it vis-à-vis Japan.

The Cabinet's decision was in essence an endorsement of Hoare's "double policy." Britain would publicly reaffirm her loyalty to League obligations, but would take no lead in proposing sanctions and do nothing in which the French would not join.

These qualifications, of course, were not part of the public announcement that League obligations would be fulfilled, and the Government now proceeded to handle the matter in a manner which gave a misleading impression of the lengths to which it was prepared to go. With the full approval of both Baldwin and Neville Chamberlain, Hoare prepared a speech for delivery at the September session of the Assembly of the League, the content and purposes of which he later described as follows:

> *The success of the speech seemed to me to depend upon whether or not I could give the League some kind of future programme. . . . There might still, I thought, be a chance of putting new life into its crippled body. I accordingly determined to make a revivalist appeal to the Assembly. At best, it might start a new chapter of League recovery, at worst, it might deter Mussolini by a display of League fervor. If there was any element of bluff in it, it was a moment when bluff was not only legitimate but inescapable.*

So disposed, Hoare left for Geneva on September 9, and, during the next two days, had lengthy private discussions with Laval, in the course of which it was agreed that, come what might, the idea of war with Italy was to be totally excluded "as too dangerous and double-edged for the future of Europe." The two likewise agreed that any sanctions which might be invoked should not be of such a type as to "provoke Mussolini into open hostility"; closing the Suez Canal was accordingly ruled out, as well as military or naval sanctions, such as a blockade of Italian ports.

Then, with these limits on action privately settled with Laval, on September 12 Hoare mounted the tribune of the Assembly and delivered himself of a pro-League speech, so categorically and even stirringly phrased that it was indeed "heard round the world":

> *On behalf of His Majesty's Government in the United Kingdom I can say that . . . they will be second to none to fulfill, within the measure of their capacity, the obligations which the Covenant lays upon them. . . . In conformity with its precise and explicit obligations, the League stands, and my country stands with it, for the collective maintenance of the Covenant in its entirety, and particularly for steady and collective resistance to all acts of unprovoked aggression.*

Brave words indeed, but they were a bluff, and failed to fool the intended target. Unawed, Mussolini rejected the compromise proposals put forward by the League, and a few weeks later launched the invasion of Ethiopia. But Hoare had succeeded admirably in fooling not only the League but his own countrymen as well. In Geneva, the Dutch delegate excitedly proclaimed: "The British have decided to stop Mussolini, even if that means using force." Vacationing on the Riviera, Winston Churchill was "stirred" as he read Hoare's speech, and thought it had "united all those forces in Britain which stood for a fearless combination of righteousness and strength." In London, Baldwin authorized the Navy to send the giant battle cruisers *Hood* and *Renown*, with numerous smaller warships, to Gibraltar. And when De Bono's troops crossed the Ethiopian frontier, the League promptly branded Italy as an aggressor who had violated the Covenant, and resolved to take collective action against her by way of sanctions.

Now all eyes turned toward London and, given Laval's attitude and their own determination to avoid war, the Baldwin government was on the spot. Indulging the hope that mild economic sanctions might check the Duce, the Cabinet sent Eden to Geneva with instructions to take no initiative, but to co-operate with the League Committee charged with the shaping and administration of sanctions. The committee shortly adopted a program comprising various financial and trade restrictions which became effective in November.

For two months the hollowness of the British policy was not apparent, and Baldwin rode to a smashing victory at the November elections, on a platform of fidelity to the League, rearmament, and collective security. But the sanctions had no visible effect on Mussolini's belligerency in Ethiopia, though the Italian advance soon ground to a halt. Meanwhile, some members of the League were growing restive over the ineffectiveness of the sanctions so far declared. The Canadian delegate proposed an embargo on oil shipments to Italy, and a meeting of the League Committee, to consider the matter, was scheduled for mid-December.

At this crucial juncture, the Chiefs of Staff, and especially Admiral Chatfield, again raised their voices to counsel caution. Their views were reinforced by a Defence Requirements Committee report, adopted November 21, which casts light on the services' distrust of collective security as a basis for British policy. In pre-League days, it was pointed out, Britain could choose for herself when and where to bring her military power to bear. Under no circumstances would she have contemplated confrontations with friendly Japan or Italy over their behavior in Manchuria or Ethiopia, remote as these lands were from vital British interests. Now, however, under the regime of collective security, Covenant obligations might, at any moment and unexpectedly, pull Britain into conflicts in which she had little direct interest and for which no military preparations had been previously thought necessary. Rather drily, the Cabinet was reminded that in November 1933 it had approved a CID [Committee of Imperial Defence] recommendation that no money be spent on defensive measures useful only against France, the United States, or Italy. Now, only two years later, defensive measures against Italy had to be hastily improvised, to meet the contingency that collective security, operating through sanctions, might provoke Italy to the point of war. And this was happening, they stressed, at a time when Japan was stirring ominously and Germany was rearming feverishly. The specter of simultaneous hostilities with two, let alone all three, of these countries was simply not to be contemplated in military terms, and must surely be avoided.

On December 2, the Cabinet met to decide what should be done. Neville Chamberlain and Eden were ready to see the oil sanctions put into effect; Hoare, Runciman, and the service representatives were unhappy at the prospect. As Foreign Secretary, Hoare took the lead in the discussions and expressed fear that oil sanctions would be *too* effective and might force Mussolini into a "mad dog" act. However, the League Committee strongly favored oil sanctions, and Britain, having pledged full support of the League, could not afford to appear obstructive. The best thing to do would be to "press on with the peace negotiations as rapidly as possible" and to hope that they might go well enough to warrant postponing the oil sanctions. Hoare then revealed that, for reasons of health, he was going to Zuoz in Switzerland for a rest and that he proposed en route to stop in Paris "to see M. Laval and to try and press on his talks with him." All this the Cabinet approved and so laid the scene for the ill-fated Hoare-Laval agreement.

Historians of the period have often attributed the fiasco to Hoare's illness and Laval's overreaching. To be sure, Hoare was far from well, but he was not seriously disabled, and indeed was planning to recoup his health at Zuoz by figure skating, at which he was expert. Hoare had made it plain, both in Cabinet and in the House, that he hoped to achieve a negotiated settlement that would obviate the need for further sanctions, and that is precisely what he tried to do. In Paris he was supported by Vansittart, who, so far from "happening" to be in Paris, or being "drawn into the affair" (as Winston Churchill put it in *The Gathering Storm*), had gone there (as Vansittart himself informed the French Ambassador in London, on the morning of his departure) "to take part in the conversations with M. Laval which the Secretary of State was about to initiate."

As Vansittart viewed the prospects in his talk with the French Ambassador, Charles Corbin, the problem "was one of finding reasonable and even generous terms to Italy, bearing in mind that it was only possible owing to the special nature of the case and that Italy was, in fact, an aggressor." All this was duly reported by Vansittart to his colleagues in a Cabinet memorandum, with the further observation: "There must therefore be an obvious limit to appetite on the one side and connivance on the other"—and connivance was a very good word to describe the program which he and Hoare now framed with Laval, to cajole the Duce into laying down his arms.

And so Hoare went on to Switzerland "well satisfied" with the agreement which he and Laval initialed on December 8, proposing a settlement involving large territorial cessions and economic concessions to Italy, and a corridor to the sea for Ethiopia. Eden and Baldwin, when they learned the terms, thought them far too generous to Italy, but what Hoare had done was generally in line with the policy approved by the Cabinet on December 2, and on the ninth the Cabinet approved the proposals in principle and directed that the British Ambassador in Addis Ababa be instructed to urge Haile Selassie to accept them.

As a piece of *Realpolitik*, there was much to be said for the Hoare-Laval proposals, and their weakness was that no one but Hoare and Laval had been thinking in those terms. Hoare's own speech in September, and Baldwin's election campaign in November, had been based on the Covenant and collective security, and the League members, the British people, and indeed most of the interested world public had come to view the matter from that standpoint. It was an impossible basis for a settlement under which the nation condemned as an aggressor was to be substantially rewarded for its aggressions. Baldwin and his colleagues failed to perceive the inevitable and disastrous consequences of the imbalance. In this failure there is great blame, and it is unfair to visit the bulk of it on Hoare.

That unhappy man had blacked out while skating and broken his nose on the ice. By the time of his return to London on December 16, his plan was dead, and he and Laval were widely regarded as a pair of swindlers. The enormously influential editor of the *Times*, Geoffrey Dawson, who had strongly backed Hoare for the foreign affairs portfolio, now urged him to resign and wrote an editorial ridiculing the proposed Ethiopian corridor to the sea as a "corridor for camels," since Laval had inserted a stipulation that no railroad should be put through the corridor, in order to protect the French-controlled railway from Addis Ababa to Djibouti. And on December 18 the same Cabinet that had approved his plan on the ninth in substance demanded that Hoare resign.

He did so at once and was replaced by Eden, who had consistently favored a much tougher policy toward Italy. But the Hoare-Laval proposals had effectively undermined Britain's leadership at Geneva, and it was too late to retrieve the situation. American participation in an oil embargo was more than doubtful, and this factor, coupled with French delaying tactics, caused the League Committee to refer the oil sanctions proposals to a committee of experts, who reported in February that, if rigorously observed and if the United States did not increase its exports to Italy, sanctions might be effective in three months' time. On February 26, 1936, Baldwin and Eden were able to persuade the Cabinet, over the dissents of Eyres-Monsell and Runciman, that Britain should support the application of oil sanctions.

But when the League Committee met early in March, Pierre Flandin (Laval's successor as Foreign Minister) succeeded, with Eden's reluctant acquiescence, in obtaining a week's postponement to make another attempt at conciliation. Before the week was out, the Germans marched into the Rhineland, and the question of oil sanctions was drowned in a sea of other troubles. On April 22, Eden reported to the Cabinet that at Geneva "hardly anyone had been thinking of Abyssinia," and gave voice to his own doubts that it "was possible to make collective security work in Europe so long as the two dictators, Mussolini and Hitler, dominated the situation." Less than three weeks later, Badoglio was in Addis Ababa and the Italian Empire was proclaimed.

Until early June, Eden succeeded, over the objections of several of his colleagues, in keeping the existing sanctions in effect, hoping that Mussolini could be induced to give public promises about his future policies in Ethiopia that might save Britain and the League a bit of face. But the Duce was not disposed to be cooperative, and on June 10, Neville Chamberlain, who in the past had supported Eden, made a public speech describing the continuance of sanctions as "the very midsummer of madness." A week later, on Eden's own recommendation, the Cabinet agreed that "the policy of the Government should be to take the initiative at the League of Nations in proposing the raising of sanctions against Italy." On July 6, after hearing a dramatic plea by Emperor Haile Selassie, now a fugitive from the Italian presence in his country, the Assembly of the League voted to lift the sanctions.

So ended one of the most disastrous passages in the history of British statecraft. In retrospect, it seems plain that the wisest course, if bold, would have been to play the game of collective security to the hilt and bring Mussolini down, even if it meant a war, in which Italy would have had no allies. But benefit might also have been derived from a more cautious, if cynical, policy of keeping the Duce on the side of the angels in Europe by allowing him a bit of deviltry in Africa.

The vice of the British policy was that it was a little of both and not enough of either. It should have been realized from the outset that ineffective sanctions would be far worse than none at all. The error was compounded by marshaling world opinion behind the banner of the Covenant and then proposing deals that flaunted the principles Britain had herself invoked. In the upshot, Britain got the worst of all possible worlds—an arrogant, resentful Mussolini thrown into ominous combination with an increasingly confident and acquisitive Hitler, a League of Nations damaged beyond repair as an engine of collective security, and a national image badly tarnished at home and abroad. "I have never before heard a British Minister . . . come down to the House of Commons and say that Britain was beaten . . . and that we must abandon an enterprise we had taken in hand," declared David Lloyd George in the House debate on lifting the sanctions, adding, as he pointed to the Government front bench: "Tonight we have had the cowardly surrender, and *there* are the cowards."

Maurice Cowling

The Rhineland Crisis

Maurice Cowling, Fellow of Peterhouse College, Cambridge, argues that Anthony Eden—who became foreign secretary in place of the hapless Samual Hoare—sought a recognition that the mid-1935 Stresa Front (the cooperation of Britain, France, and Italy against Germany) was dead. He desired instead "a return to normality . . . and the creation of conditions in which Hitler could behave like Stresemann," the German foreign minister in the 1920s and coauthor of the Locarno pact. When Hitler violated the Versailles treaty and sent troops into the Rhineland on March 7, 1936, neither the foreign secretary nor his colleagues were surprised by the action, though they were taken aback by its suddenness and hoped to seize the opportunity in order that "good might come out of evil." For Cowling, the crisis tells us more about the unhappy state of Anglo-French cooperation than it does about the threat to relations with the Germans.

Eden had no wish to quarrel with Hitler. While half-expecting "foreign adventures" as a way of "distracting attention from . . . [economic] failures at home," he regarded them as "an additional reason for coming to terms quickly."

Eden's appeasement raised a finely-aimed combination of expectations. His long-term objective was League-based disarmament. But this would only be possible if short-term rearmament was effected first. Short-term rearmament was necessary in order to prevent Hitler taking steps to make *détente* or disarmament possible. Since this would be greatly disliked "by an important section

From *The Impact of Hitler: British Politics and British Policy, 1933–1940*, 1975, pp. 105–108. Reprinted by permission of Cambridge University Press.

of British opinion" it was essential, therefore, "so far as the home front is concerned," to make a "renewed attempt at a political settlement."

Eden was not aiming to resist any particular act of aggression. He had wanted to defeat Mussolini because a victory for "the League principle" would facilitate "a political settlement in Europe." But he did not want Anglo-French, or British, involvement in a Franco-Russian alliance against Germany, and he resented the Abyssinian somersaults of the French as much as he resented those of his critics in the Cabinet. One reason why oil sanctions receded in the New Year was his refusal to promise Flandin reciprocal co-operation in Europe. One reason why he was unwilling to do this was his belief that it would be unnecessary if Mussolini could be checked in Abyssinia.

What Eden had to do was to recognise that Stresa was dead. What he wanted instead was a return to the normality of the twenties and the creation of conditions in which Hitler could behave like Stresemann. This would involve major adjustments and a major effort to bring institutional arrangements in line with the realities of power. It would remove the impression which Hoare had created and confirm the moral centrality of the Conservative position. By the time of the next election (in 1940), success might be in sight, he thought, after a three-year haul in the course of which Hitler would remilitarise the Rhineland, have "one or more" of the ex-German colonies and benefit from economic priority along the Danube in return for signing a disarmament convention, joining a reconstructed League and renouncing further territorial claims in Africa and Europe.

Nor was this affected by March 7. That Hitler would put armies into the demilitarised Rhineland had been expected for a long time before he did it. When the Cabinet had discussed the possibility after Flandin asked it to, it agreed that, since "neither France nor England was . . . in a position to take effective military action," its Locarno obligations should be swallowed up in discussion of a general settlement. This was swallowed up by Hitler's action two days later.

Eden described the *coup* as discrediting Hitler's peaceful protestations. But he said that "good" might come out of "evil," that the Rhineland might have been conceded in negotiation and that it was desirable to promote a "far-reaching settlement."

When faced with the occupation, the Cabinet talked in a way which frightened Baldwin. But the outcome was an earlier opportunity of discussing a settlement than there would otherwise have been. Eden was sent, at Flandin's request, to a meeting of the Locarno powers in Paris, where he was asked to support a public demand for withdrawal on pain of war. On his return to London, the Cabinet allowed him to approach Hitler secretly with a view to persuading him to withdraw pending discussions about the future. When this was leaked to the newspapers, his main object at the League and Locarno meetings in London was to defuse the conflict.

Eden had no desire to go to war. His policy was the Cabinet's policy of avoiding war while trying to "avoid a repudiation of Locarno." Such firmness as he displayed was designed to anticipate Flandin's demands for more; none of it was intended to be turned into action.

The question was not, in fact, put in terms of action; the French claim was that the threat to act would be enough to be effective. But, whereas he was prepared to push the Cabinet where his own threats were concerned (in Abyssinia), Eden did nothing to press it about the Rhineland.

In restraining Flandin, Eden was conditioned by defence deficiencies, by the damage a German crisis would do to sanctions against Italy and by the Conservative party's refusal to go to war. He was also moved by the belief, which Flandin sometimes confirmed, that French firmness was designed for public consumption in France.

After his isolated approach to Hitler, Eden aimed to persuade Belgium to restrain Flandin, whose position at the beginning of the London meeting was that troops sent to the Rhineland since March 7 "should be withdrawn before negotiations for a settlement were begun." Though van Zeeland wanted Locarno procedures activated if Hitler refused guarantees for the future, his demands were a great deal less extensive. He and Flandin were both pulled back when Eden "insisted on the importance of constructive negotiations for the new Europe" and "could not agree to fight a war to drive Germany out of the demilitarized zone" if it was to be handed back as part of a settlement.

This first erosion was followed by a French proposal that the Hague Court should be asked to decide whether Locarno and the Franco-Soviet pact were incompatible. This was accompanied by a Cabinet decision that Hitler should be asked to send a senior person to London to be on hand while the other powers discussed the German action.

From March 13 British policy was conducted by Eden, Halifax and Chamberlain in the shadow of brooding negatives from Baldwin and unsuccessful attempts by MacDonald to "thrust himself into [the] team." By March 16 they had sold Flandin and van Zeeland the idea of an international force on both sides of the French and German frontiers. Though Flandin was told that a German refusal would "harden British opinion" against Hitler, the point was not to harden British opinion but to remove any excuse for verbal belligerence and "get the 5 Locarno Powers (including Germany) round the table."

In spite of Flandin, the British government emerged a fortnight after the occupation of the Rhineland without having honoured existing commitments, without having gained new ones and having "rather limited than extended our commitments under Locarno." When Hitler then restored tension by rejecting all short-term proposals about the demilitarised zone, Eden aimed to postpone discussion of the major issues until the French elections relieved Flandin, or his successor, of the need to yield to pressure.

In aiming once more at restraint, Eden asked the Cabinet to reaffirm the Locarno position and propose staff talks with France and Belgium about the "technical conditions" necessary to meeting it. Despite doubts about the public's reaction, the Cabinet agreed. On March 26, there was a successful parliamentary debate in which, for the first time since March 7, by being firm themselves Eden and Chamberlain elicited a demonstration of conciliatory firmness towards Germany.

These acts of reassurance did nothing to satisfy the French who fixed on the fortification of the demilitarised zone (if that occurred) as a ground for Locarno sanctions against Germany. Eden denied the Locarno powers' authority to impose sanctions and questioned their ability to enforce them. On April 22 he persuaded Flandin that there should be no further Locarno meeting until the French elections were over.

By this time Hitler had made no concessions about the Rhineland and had justified the occupation on the ground that the Franco-Soviet alliance was a threat to German security. In response to the British suggestion, he had sent both Ribbentrop and a *Peace Plan* to London. Their arrival (on April 1) enabled Eden to claim that conciliation was going on when sanctions were rejected. It was his promise to send a probing reply which enabled Flandin to agree that the Locarno meeting should be postponed.

The defusing of the Rhineland situation without an Anglo-French confrontation was, doubtless, a triumph for British diplomacy. But the occupation had not been, and nothing that had been done had improved the credit of the League. When it was further damaged by the Italian victory in Abyssinia, collapse was complete.

Larry William Fuchser

The Anschluss

Larry William Fuchser, author of a critical study of appeasement policy, *Neville Chamberlain and Appeasement*, writes that the prime minister was little surprised at the *Anschluss* of Germany and Austria in March 1938 but was deeply concerned about the method chosen to carry it off. According to Fuchser, Chamberlain—who had replaced Baldwin in May 1937—saw the crisis not as evidence of a need for stiffer resistance to Hitler but as proof of the necessity for redoubled efforts to seek a settlement with Germany. Rather than signs of weakness, the author sees in Chamberlain's determination and resistance to opposition clear evidence of his mastery over the government and its policy.

From the privacy of his study, Chamberlain watched with growing concern the ominous new developments in Germany. He admitted that these events had come as an almost total surprise to the British policymakers and significantly complicated the diplomatic situation. Although he was decidedly apprehensive about the future direction of German policy, he thought that, at least in the short run, German military capability had been diminished. His feeling of apprehension was no doubt compounded by Henderson's warning that "Hitler was contemplating some immediate action about Austria."

Therefore, when German armies began crossing the Austrian frontier on the morning of 12 March Chamberlain was not particularly surprised. In fact, he had written to his sisters stating that there had been many signs of an impending Nazi takeover of Austria but that he had wished this could be effected peacefully. As early as 19 February, Chamberlain had told the Cabinet that "it was difficult to believe" that the eventual result of German policy "would not be the absorption of Austria and probably some action in Czechoslovakia." Whether by carefully premeditated plan or by pragmatic opportunism, Hitler's armies were, despite initial blundering and ill planning, soon in occupation of the whole of Austria. What was once a sovereign member of the League was now an administrative subdivision of the German Reich. The British, having once again been presented with a *fait accompli*, were forced to reevaluate the premises on which their policy had heretofore been based.

Clearly, what concerned Chamberlain and his cadre of supporters was not the fact of Austria's destruction but the method by which it was achieved. In fact, during the brief crisis leading up to the Anschluss, the Government had given Hitler every reason to assume that the British, however much they might abhor military action, would do nothing to oppose it. After Austrian Prime Minister Schuschnigg had announced his intention to hold a plebiscite*

* On March 9, 1938, Kurt Schuschnigg announced a plebiscite to be held four days later on the issue of continued Austrian independence from Germany. In part fearing the result of the balloting, Hitler sent German troops into Austria on the eleventh.

and German military action to prevent it had become a possibility, Halifax had informed Ribbentrop that "the threat of force was an intolerable method." But Chamberlain, leaving no doubt as to Britain's intentions, added that the two countries "could begin working in earnest towards a German-British understanding once we had all got past this unpleasant affair." In Berlin, Henderson made it clear that he agreed with Goering that Dr. Schuschnigg "had acted with precipitate folly." These were hardly the sort of statements which might have deterred Hitler from advancing into Austria. . . .

The principal effect of the Anschluss on Chamberlain's view of continental affairs was that it caused him to redouble his efforts at reaching a negotiated settlement with the Axis powers. At the same time, however, he believed that the British should demonstrate their resolve by making a public announcement of an increase in the rearmament program. Chamberlain also wanted to undertake private conversations with the Italians. Everyone involved in foreign policy formulation, including Chamberlain, believed that if Hitler were planning a new aggressive move it would be toward Czechoslovakia, with a view to incorporating the Sudeten Germans into the Reich. Chamberlain himself told the Cabinet that ". . . if we can avoid another violent coup in Czechoslovakia, which ought to be feasible, it may be possible for Europe to settle down again and some day for us to start peace talks with the Germans." The incorporation of Austria into the German Reich was no doubt a setback for the prime minister's policy, although not an insurmountable one. In fact, Chamberlain was even able to interpret events so as to vindicate his own views. "What a fool Roosevelt would have looked if he had launched his precious proposal," he told the Cabinet, and "what would he have thought of us if we had encouraged him to publish it, as Anthony was so eager to do and how we too would have made ourselves the laughing stock of the world."

Reactions to the Anschluss

Chamberlain's personal interpretation of the meaning to be attached to the Anschluss was clear and unequivocal. While a show of British strength might serve a useful purpose, the better option was a redoubled effort toward reaching a negotiated Anglo-German settlement. Of this, Chamberlain was absolutely certain. Therefore, his first task was to insure that the Cabinet would not interfere.

On 12 March, Chamberlain opened the emergency meeting of the Cabinet by saying that although there was probably not very much that could be done, he had thought the Cabinet should meet. The tone of the Cabinet minutes of that meeting leaves no doubt that in foreign affairs the prime minister was calling all the shots. It was equally clear that the Cabinet had been supplanted by the Foreign Policy Committee [FPC] as the forum for the making of policy.

The emergency session was merely an occasion for Chamberlain to interpret to the Cabinet the meaning of events in Central Europe. He told his colleagues that Germany's actions were "most distressing and shocking to the world" and that they "made international appeasement much more difficult."

> *In spite of all, however, he [i.e., Chamberlain] felt that this thing had to come. Nothing short of an overwhelming display of force would have stopped it. Herr Hitler had been planning to take this action for some time and Dr. Schuschnigg's blunder had given him the chance. . . . So he believed that what had happened was inevitable unless the Powers had been able to say, "If you make war on Austria you will have to deal with us." At any rate the question was now out of the way.*

Chamberlain told the Cabinet that he believed some announcement about increasing the rate of rearmament was appropriate and that this increase should be in the air force and in anti-aircraft defenses, but he wanted the announcement to be made at a later date. For the moment, he warned the Cabinet "against giving the impression that the country was faced with the prospect of war within a few weeks." This was all that Chamberlain asked of the Cabinet. No collective Cabinet decisions were to be made and there was to be no discussion of the future direction of British policy or the alternatives available. Such matters were decided elsewhere.

The following day, on 15 March, at a meeting of the FPC, Chamberlain began to clear the way for new initiatives. He did not ask for, nor accept, advice from his colleagues. The form and substance of these new initiatives had already been worked out between the prime minister and the foreign secretary. The FPC meeting was for appearances only, so that Chamberlain could present his own policy to the full Cabinet as the product of supposedly long and exhaustive deliberations by a specialized body of the Cabinet. It was also useful in that the deliberations were a device by which Chamberlain's policy could be made more acceptable to the Commons and to public opinion in general. Chamberlain clearly recognized that the Anschluss had strengthened the hand of his political opponents within the Tory party and he therefore needed a solid core of support within the Government to proceed.

The first matter to be settled was the effect of the Anschluss on Anglo-Italian relations. Theoretically at least, the Italian offer to open conversations was still in effect. So also was Eden's previous pledge that the opening of talks should be linked to a withdrawal of Italian troops from Spain. In fact, Chamberlain had reaffirmed this pledge in the Commons on 21 February. Now, privately in the FPC, he repudiated that pledge, saying that he "did not think that . . . the Government were necessarily pledged to the view that the Spanish question must be settled before the Anglo-Italian Agreement could be executed."

Nevertheless, Chamberlain told the FPC of his intention to inform Ciano "that Hitler's recent action in regard to Austria, had made it very much more difficult for the British Government to make an agreement with Italy." Moreover, Chamberlain told the Committee that the Anschluss had greatly strengthened the hand of those in Britain who opposed conversations with the dictators. In conclusion, Chamberlain said,

> *He did not think anything that had happened should cause the Government to alter their present policy, on the contrary, recent events had confirmed him in his opinion that that policy was a right one and he only regretted that it had not been adopted earlier. He agreed, however, that recent events had greatly disturbed public opinion and that the Government's policy would have to be explained and justified to public opinion ever more carefully and thoroughly than would otherwise have been necessary.*

Chamberlain thus recognized that the Anschluss made it impossible to renege on the public pledge not to conclude an agreement with Italy without first attaining a settlement of the Spanish question. The implication of Chamberlain's words was indisputable; the prime minister was quite prepared to reach an agreement with Italy on the best terms possible even without a clear sign of Italian good faith. He said, "Ciano should also be told that if Italy sincerely wished for an Anglo-Italian agreement, he must assist us to get over the bad reactions on public opinion of Hitler's actions for which he recognised of course neither Italy nor himself were in any way responsible." Taken literally, Chamberlain's statement seemed to imply that he, at least, believed that the Government had more in common with the Italians than with their own opposition.

Government policy, as articulated in the secrecy of the Foreign Policy Committee, was now rapidly diverging from policy articulated by the Tory Opposition led by Winston Churchill. In the House of Commons, meeting in the wake of the Anschluss, Churchill, in the somber and prophetic tones for which he has become justly famous, called for a "grand alliance to arrest this approaching war." While Churchill deliberately avoided making an open break with the Government, a grand alliance was hardly a policy which Chamberlain would favor. For the time being at least, Chamberlain felt secure enough to proceed along independent lines and safely ignore rising opposition from both the left and the right. In fact, the strength of Chamberlain's parliamentary mandate would remain secure until well after Munich.

In the meantime, the most significant discussion of foreign policy options was taking place outside the public forum. On 18 March, Halifax presented to the Foreign Policy Committee a memo in which he set forth the alternatives open to Britain with regard to Germany and the Sudeten question. The foreign secretary reminded the Cabinet that Britain's only existing commitment to Czechoslovakia was that of one League member to another. However, France had signed a treaty with Czechoslovakia in 1925 in which each country had pledged itself to come to the other's aid in the event of unprovoked aggression by Germany. In addition, in 1935 the Soviet Union had signed a similar treaty with Czechoslovakia, but one in which it was specified that the treaty would become operative only if France came to the assistance of

Czechoslovakia as the victim of aggression. To the British and Chamberlain in particular, these treaties looked all too similar to the web of entangling alliances which had existed in 1914. Therefore, the dilemma was one of extraordinary delicacy. Any attempt by Britain to deter Germany in the Sudetenland would involve an additional British commitment to Czechoslovakia, a commitment which appeared exceedingly dangerous.

Halifax submitted that there were basically three alternatives open to Britain. The first was a grand alliance against the dictators as advocated by Churchill. The second was a renewed commitment to France which would, because of the Franco-Czech treaty, be an indirect guarantee to Czechoslovakia. The third was to do nothing in the way of increasing British commitments and to encourage the Czechs to make the best terms possible with the Germans.

Both Chamberlain and Halifax left little doubt which of these alternatives they preferred. To the FPC, Chamberlain gave his assessment of Hitler's intentions with regard to Czechoslovakia, saying that it "might be rash to forecast what Germany would do, but at the same time the seizure of Czechoslovakia would not be in accordance with Hitler's policy which was to include all Germans in the Reich but not to include other nationalities." It seemed likely "that Germany would absorb the Sudeten German territory and reduce the rest of Czechoslovakia to a condition of dependent neutrality." Hankey reminded the Committee that for economic reasons Czechoslovakia "could not exist as a separate political and economic entity." Inskip felt that the country was a highly artificial residue of the Treaty of Versailles and that he "could see no reason why we should take any steps to maintain such a unit in being."

Chamberlain's only reservation to the Halifax proposal was to suggest that it was not enough merely to approach the Czechs with the suggestion that they meet German demands. He wanted a concurrent approach to Germany which would involve that country in the negotiations. This, he said, "would have the advantage that it would secure permanency." With regard to France, both Halifax and Chamberlain noted that Britain "could not afford to see France overrun." By avoiding any further continental commitment, Britain would retain her freedom of action and avoid automatic involvement in a continental conflict. The great advantage of this strategy of action was, of course, that Britain could keep both France and Germany guessing.

With the full force of the combined Chamberlain-Halifax arguments, the outcome of the FPC deliberations was a foregone conclusion. The three options presented by the foreign secretary were the only alternatives considered. There was very little debate; no one supported the idea of a grand alliance. A few expressed their support for France, but their arguments carried little conviction. The Chamberlain-Halifax line was accepted.

As he presented his case to the Committee, no other conclusions than those Chamberlain himself had arrived at seemed possible. As he said,

> *. . . the more one studied the map of central Europe the more hopeless was the idea that any effective help could be swiftly brought to Czechoslovakia in an emergency. . . . It followed therefore, that we should have to say that it was impracticable effectively to aid Czechoslovakia in time and that all we could do would be to make war on Germany, but we were in no position from the armament point of view to enter such a war and in his . . . opinion it would be most dangerous for us to do so.*

To support Czechoslovakia meant war, a war for which Britain was ill-prepared. Interestingly enough, neither Chamberlain nor anyone else raised the possibility that Germany might be deterred from attacking Czechoslovakia by a renewed British commitment to that country.

Chamberlain said that France's domestic political situation meant that she was "in a hopeless position" to make war on Germany. Therefore, Chamberlain said he would have thought, ". . . the policy of France would have been directed to giving us wholehearted support in an attempt to find a peaceful solution, to avoid any risk of an outbreak of war and to reestablish the confidence of Europe which had been shattered by recent events." Chamberlain said that he ". . . did not think that Germany would resent representations by us that the Sudeten problem should be settled by negotiations between Czechoslovakia and herself though she would no doubt strongly resent any suggestion that that question should be settled for her by foreigners." Chamberlain went on to say:

> *If Germany could obtain her desiderata by peaceful methods there was no reason to suppose she would reject such a procedure in favour of one based on violence. It should be noted that throughout the Austrian adventure Herr Hitler had studiously refrained from saying or doing anything to provoke us and in small matters such as passport and exchange facilities for British subjects returning home from Austria consideration had been shown. All this did not look as if Germany wished to antagonise us, on the contrary, it indicated a desire to keep on good terms with us.*

Thus it was that, less than a week after the Anschluss, without seeking military advice, in opposition to the Foreign Office, without consulting France, and in almost complete ignorance of Soviet attitudes, the Foreign Policy Committee accepted Chamberlain's policy and abandoned any attempt to resist further German aggression in Czechoslovakia.

The policy, it should be noted, was not merely a passive one of doing nothing to resist Hitler but rather a positive move in anticipation of what was believed to be the future course of German policy. Rather than wait on events, the British were committing themselves to a policy of urging the Czechs to compromise before Hitler sought a solution by force. It need scarcely be noted that internal Czechoslovakian politics had nothing whatever to do with that decision.

The following day, after the basic decisions had been taken, the Committee was given the advice of the chiefs of staff. The military chiefs concluded that nothing the allies could possibly do could prevent Germany from overrunning all of Czechoslovakia, and if this happened, Italy and Japan would probably seize the opportunity to further their own end, and the result would be world war. The chiefs of staff's report was a convenient support for the Chamberlain line and persuasive evidence which could be used to gain acceptance by the Cabinet.

In presenting the FPC decision to the full Cabinet, Halifax said that both he and the prime minister had been inclined to favor the idea of a grand alliance, but that upon hearing the report from the chiefs of staff, they had concluded, and the FPC with them, that the best course would be to try to "induce the Government of Czechoslovakia to apply themselves to producing a direct settlement with the Sudeten Deutsch" and to "persuade the French to use their influence to obtain such a settlement." Halifax said that "it was a disagreeable business which had to be done as pleasantly as possible. . . ." Chamberlain reiterated Halifax's arguments, adding, ". . . it was difficult to believe, however, that if the subject were discussed seriously between the two nations, the French would not be glad to find some method to relieve them of their engagement." Chamberlain emphasized the importance of reaching an agreement with Italy, adding, ". . . the conversations in Rome were proceeding with almost embarrassing ease and rapidity. . . ." With even less discussion than in the FPC, the Cabinet accepted the Chamberlain-Halifax line. . . .

Chamberlain had begun by gaining acceptance for his views in the narrowest possible forum. In persuading his colleagues in the FPC, Chamberlain had gained *de facto* allies in the larger Cabinet. Having acquiesced in the FPC, a colleague could not very well oppose Chamberlain in the full Cabinet. The same principle applied to the larger government forum. Once the Cabinet had decided on a policy, the price of public opposition in the Commons was resignation. At this level, a dissident minister had to deal with the Eden dilemma; that is, for resignation to be politically credible, the minister must articulate an alternative course of action, and this, unfortunately, no one in the Government was either willing or able to do. Such was the meaning of Chamberlain's comment that his political strategy had always been first to make up his own mind as to the correct option to be pursued and then to persuade his colleagues by taking them step by step through his own decision-making process. It was a supremely effective strategy.

Chamberlain wrote that his speech in the Commons had been an enormous victory and that he could not recall that any British statesman had ever made a crucial policy statement that had been as widely acclaimed as his own. While such claims were no doubt exaggerated, it does seem fairly certain that then, as at the time of Munich, the vague and ill-defined force known as public opinion was squarely behind the prime minister. While Chamberlain no doubt misread German intentions and saw reasonableness where there was none, there can be little doubt that he understood full well the dynamics of British domestic politics and the degree to which he could make policy independent of traditional constitutional constraint. In sum, he had correctly assessed the weakness of the opposition and the strength of his own position. It is therefore no great exaggeration to say that the country lay in the palm of his hand.

In the midst of this flurry of activity, Chamberlain's letters reveal the private feelings of a master politician. With an imminent fascist victory in Spain, with the persistent political instability in France (whose government Chamberlain suspected of having secret contacts with the British left), with the conniving Russians attempting to involve the British in a European war, with all these dangers to deal with, Chamberlain felt that the Opposition's cry for a more bold and coherent policy was more than a little unfair. The idea of a grand alliance had, he wrote, occurred to him long before Churchill's speech. Indeed, Chamberlain wrote, the idea had everything in its favor except that it was simply not feasible. After reviewing the arguments concerning the indefensibility of Czechoslovakia, he concluded that he had virtually given up any idea of a formal pledge to Czechoslovakia or of a pledge to France with respect to her treaty commitments to that nation.

Even before his speech in the Commons of 24 March, Chamberlain's mind was moving ahead to even bolder measures. In a letter to his sister, Chamberlain confided that he was thinking of a new approach to Hitler to follow up on previous overtures by Halifax and Henderson. His idea was to remind Hitler that he had been warned that military action against Austria would have the most adverse effects on the British public. Therefore Hitler had no one to blame but himself for the bellicose criticism he was receiving. Moreover, Hitler's action had thus virtually precluded any further discussion of a colonial settlement.

But Chamberlain was willing to let bygones be bygones and believed that together they could work on repairing the damage. He would remind the German leader that the British public believed Hitler was about to attack Czechoslovakia and that no one would believe his protestations to the contrary. Chamberlain said that he would ask Hitler to tell him precisely what he wanted for the Sudeten Deutsch and that if Hitler's demands were well-founded, Britain would urge the Czechs to acquiesce in return for a German pledge of no further involvement. Chamberlain noted that if Hitler would play along, he might be willing to join in an Anglo-German guarantee of Czechoslovakia. While he was not sure he was willing to go quite this far, Chamberlain wrote that he believed he had at least a plan for opening negotiations, a plan to which Hitler might be receptive.

Having once committed himself to the notion of an Anglo-German guarantee of Czechoslovakia it was but a short step to the idea of a meeting between Chamberlain and Hitler in which a joint agreement could be negotiated and then forced upon the Czech people. Just as in the case of Abyssinia, the wishes of the peoples involved and the moral question of the possible destruction of a sovereign state mattered hardly at all. The important thing to Chamberlain was that these changes be accomplished peaceably. Nor was Chamberlain particularly concerned with the fate of the Czech people in the event of a German attack, or with the strategic indefensibility of a Czech state in which the Sudetenland passed to German control. What concerned him above all else was his belief that German aggression would inevitably lead to the involvement of Britain in another world war. Long before he became prime minister, the course he would follow had been settled in Chamberlain's mind. The post-Anschluss deliberations did little more than insure that his view of British policy and his alone would prevail.

Neville Chamberlain

We Could Not Help Czechoslovakia

Neville Chamberlain wrote hundreds of remarkably candid letters to his two unmarried sisters, Hilda and Ida, during his political career; many contain useful insights into his thinking. In this brief example, written March 20, 1938, the prime minister made it clear that he had no intention of risking war to attempt quixotically to save Czechoslovakia from the German grasp.

With Franco winning in Spain by the aid of German guns and Italian planes, with a French government in which one cannot have the slightest confidence and which I suspect to be in closest touch with our Opposition, with the Russians stealthily and cunningly pulling the strings behind the scenes to get us involved in war with Germany (our Secret Service doesn't spend all its time looking out of the window), and finally with a Germany flushed with triumph, and all too conscious of her power, the prospect looked black indeed. In face of such problems, to be badgered and pressed to come out and give a clear, decided, bold, and unmistakable lead, show "ordinary courage," and all the rest of the twaddle, is calculated to vex a man who has to take responsibility for the consequences. As a matter of fact, the plan of the "Grand Alliance," as Winston calls it, had occurred to me long before he mentioned it. . . . I talked about it to Halifax, and we submitted it to the chiefs of staff and the F.O. [Foreign Office] experts. It is a very attractive idea; indeed, there is almost everything to be said for it until you come to examine its practicability. From that moment its attraction vanishes. You have only to look at the map to see that nothing that France or we could do could possibly save Czechoslovakia

From Neville Chamberlain Papers NC 18/1/1042. Reprinted with permission of the University of Birmingham.

from being overrun by the Germans, if they wanted to do it. The Austrian frontier is practically open; the great Skoda munition works are within easy bombing distance of the German aerodromes, the railways all pass through German territory, Russia is 100 miles away.

Therefore we could not help Czechoslovakia—she would simply be a pretext for going to war with Germany. That we could not think of unless we had a reasonable prospect of being able to beat her to her knees in a reasonable time, and of that I see no sign. I have therefore abandoned any idea of giving guarantees to Czechoslovakia, or the French in connection with her obligations to that country.

Anglo-French Conference, April 28–29, 1938

British and French Cooperation?

After the *Anschluss*, Hitler turned his attention to Czechoslovakia and the more than three million ethnic Germans of the Sudetenland. The absorption of Austria, of course, meant that the region was now bordered on three sides by the Reich. In a summit conference in London in late April, Chamberlain and Halifax made clear to Daladier and Bonnet that although the prime minister had already warned Hitler that an attack on Czechoslovakia would lead to war and, hence, possibly to unforeseen events, Britain would offer no guarantee to Czechoslovakia nor to France in aid of her mutual defense treaty with the Czechs. Despite the diplomatic language used, it is clear that both of the delegations were agreed that pressure should be put on the Czech president, Edvard Benes, to come to an agreement with the Germans. Meanwhile, Chamberlain would take it upon himself to remind Hitler of the obvious fact that he could have much of what he wished without resort to war.

From *Documents on British Foreign Policy, 1919–1939*, Third Series, Vol. I, 1949, pp. 227–232. Reprinted with permission from Her Majesty's Stationery Office.

Lord Halifax said that both sides had had an opportunity of considering further what had passed at this morning's meeting. He thought that a good deal of what had been said, both by M. Bonnet towards the end of the morning's meeting and by M. Daladier at an earlier stage, did involve the suggestion that at some point or other His Majesty's Government should combine any advice which, in conjunction with the French Government, they might give to Dr. Benes, with a guarantee to Dr. Benes that if he accepted our advice and acted upon it, he could then count upon full British support if the German Government rejected his proposals and Czechoslovakia were a victim of German aggression. He was fully sensible of the force of what M. Daladier had said in the morning regarding the importance of doing everything we could to check Germany in her process of absorption, and to prevent the establishment of a German hegemony in Europe as a result of the absorption of one unit after another. He fully realised the exact implications of what M. Daladier had said, but he could only remind him that for the reasons already given by Mr. Chamberlain it was impossible for His Majesty's Government to contemplate going any further in the way of commitments than had been indicated in the Prime Minister's speech in the House of Commons on the 24th March. A further consideration which had not been mentioned, but which would no doubt be present in the minds of the French Ministers, was that whatever might be the attitude of this country—and it was at present as the Prime Minister had described it—His Majesty's Government also had to take into account the attitude of the Dominions on a question of this kind in which they might well become involved as a consequence of whatever decision was taken now. He could, therefore, only repeat the statement made by Mr. Chamberlain at the morning meeting regarding the impossibility of making any further commitments.

This being the case, they had been asking themselves what further help they were in a position to give with a view to relieving the common anxieties felt by the French Government and also by His Majesty's Government. From their point of view they had re-examined the possibility, which had already been suggested, of making some approach both to Prague and also to Berlin. When discussing at the morning session the question of approaching Prague, M.

Daladier had said, very properly, that it was not only a question of Prague, and that it was not less important also to take steps elsewhere. It was therefore for consideration whether a useful purpose might be served if we also made an approach to Berlin, and what character such an approach should take if it were decided upon. It was possible that the German Government might take the line that the Sudeten question was their concern and not the concern of His Majesty's Government or of the French Government. We should, however, then be able to reply that Field-Marshal Göring had given His Majesty's Government certain assurances in respect of Czechoslovakia after the German absorption of Austria. Although it was true that Great Britain was not directly interested in the lot of the Sudeten Germans, she was closely interested in the peace of Europe, and it could be pointed out to the German Government that His Majesty's Government had made it plain to them that if the problems of Czechoslovakia were handled unwisely, this might lead to a European war.

The British Ministers had been wondering whether it would be wise to make an approach to Berlin in some such sense; and, if it were considered wise to act on these lines, which of two alternative courses should be adopted. The first alternative would be to approach Dr. Benes in the first place, and find out from him the utmost concessions which he was prepared to make. An approach could then be made to Berlin, in which His Majesty's Government would inform the German Government of the measures which they thought Dr. Benes might be willing to take if he were satisfied that on such lines a settlement could be reached which might be expected to endure. They would then be able to judge from the reactions to this approach what were the real intentions of Germany. Alternatively, it might be considered better to approach Berlin in the first place and say to the German Government that they had on many occasions represented that the treatment of the Sudeten Germans by the Czechoslovak Government was a matter of the gravest anxiety for them. We could say that we were also concerned over this problem in so far as we wished to see it handled in such a way as would not involve the possibility of war. We could ask the German Government to suggest what they considered to be the best means of relieving these anxieties, and of remedying what they alleged to be maltreatment of their people in Czechoslovakia. He had a feeling that German claims were rather like mushrooms, in that they grew in the dark, and if we could succeed in bringing them into the open, though there might be dangers and disadvantages in so doing, we should at least know where we were; and we should know what claims were really being made, and be on firmer ground on which to decide what action should be taken. If some such methods were considered useful, His Majesty's Government might go on to suggest to the German Government that they should look at the position in the following light. It was possible that if His Majesty's Government could persuade Dr. Benes to move so far in the direction of further concessions, the German Government might obtain 60 per cent. or 70 per cent. of their complete demands by pacific methods. If, however, they rejected such a compromise and insisted on the full 100 per cent. of their demands, then there was the gravest risk that they could only achieve their object by war, and in that event the position of the British Government had been quite clearly defined for all to read by the Prime Minister in the House of Commons on the 24th March. He felt that something on the above lines offered the best solution, and, in fact, the only compromise between M. Daladier's very natural request for a firm British commitment, which it was, however, quite impossible for His Majesty's Government to give, and the attitude of His Majesty's Government having regard to public opinion in this country and in other parts of the Empire.

M. Bonnet said that there was one question he wished to ask. If we accepted as a hypothesis that such a *démarche* [maneuver] were made in Prague and that the Czechoslovak Government agreed to offer further concessions, at that moment and under those particular circumstances would the British Government then be prepared to affirm its solidarity with the French Government with a view to the maintenance of a settlement on the lines agreed upon with Dr. Benes? He felt it was essential that when such a point had been reached we should no longer remain in the present state of uncertainty.

Lord Halifax said that, if he had rightly understood M. Bonnet, the latter had asked whether, after Dr. Benes had informed His Majesty's Government of the concessions which he was prepared to make, and the latter had found them reasonable, His Majesty's Government would then be prepared, in the event of the rejection of these concessions by Germany and of a German attack on Czechoslovakia to accept an obligation to defend Czechoslovakia against the results of such German aggression. If this was M. Bonnet's question, he could only answer that, for the reasons already given, it would be impossible to accept such a commitment.

He thought, however, that it was perhaps worth mentioning at this stage that in the view of His Majesty's Government it would be going a long way if, as he had suggested, we were to repeat direct to Herr Hitler the words which Mr. Chamberlain had already pronounced in the House of Commons regarding the attitude of this country in certain eventualities. He felt there was a great difference between repeating such words direct to the German Government and so giving it a particular application, and pronouncing them in the House of Commons primarily for our own people, even if the German Government naturally knew of them.

M. Daladier wished to recall exactly what the position of the French Government was, and to make certain concrete proposals. They considered that solidarity should be established between France and Great Britain and any other countries which were ready to join them, and we should then pursue a policy aimed at reconciliation in Czechoslovakia. It was, of course, legitimate—as the Prime Minister and Lord Halifax had suggested—first to inform ourselves and find out how far Dr. Benes's proposals were calculated to bring about a degree of appeasement desired on both sides in Czechoslovakia. If, however, the Czechoslovak Government were ready to make concessions on a reasonable scale, then he felt it was essential, as a minimum, to obtain assurances from Berlin that Germany would not resort to arms with a view to solving this question. She might be reminded of Field-Marshal Göring's assurances to the British Ambassador in Berlin that Germany had no intention of resorting to force in this connexion. He did not think there was anything in such an approach of a nature to arouse German susceptibilities. But it should be clearly realised that if, after such *démarches* had been made at Berlin and Prague, and in spite of the assurances given by Field-Marshal Göring, which he would probably be prepared to renew, Germany nevertheless resorted to force to settle the Sudeten question, then the British and French Governments would have to draw the obvious conclusions. He had framed concrete suggestions on these lines with a view, as Lord Halifax had suggested, to preventing the German mushroom growing too rapidly. There was nothing in what he had suggested to offend any Government, particularly the German Government, if their policy was loyal and sincere and they really wished to maintain the peace of Europe. He suggested that it might be possible to agree on action on these lines, and he added that the suggestions already put forward by Lord Halifax were in many respects calculated to give satisfaction to the French Government.

Mr. Chamberlain realised that there was naturally some difficulty in reaching agreement on this question, but he was not quite clear as to the precise form of the *démarche* suggested by M. Daladier. If he had understood him aright, he had seemed to commit both the British and French Governments to a particular Czechoslovak plan of concessions which might not prove acceptable to the German Government. If we were then to ask the German Government for an assurance that they would not resort to force, it was doubtful whether we should get such an assurance in the form we required. Supposing, however, that the German Government did, for the time being, accept the Czechoslovak proposals, although they did not think that they were in every way satisfactory, it would be only too easy for them at a later stage to stir up disturbances in the Sudeten areas and then intervene, saying, as they had done in the case of Austria, that they had no intention of using force, but had been compelled to take action in order to avoid unnecessary bloodshed. He was therefore a little uncomfortable of [*sic*] accepting M. Daladier's proposal at this stage without trying to obtain first from Germany some indication of what the German Government would be prepared to accept. If therefore an approach to the German Government by His Majesty's Government was desired by the French Government, His Majesty's Government would prefer to make such an approach simultaneously with their representations at Prague. His Majesty's Government would then be in a position to say that they, for their part, were doing their best to bring about a peaceful solution by representing to Dr. Benes the necessity of his contributing to such a solution.

The British Government could then add that it took two to reach an agreement and ask the German Government what their position was. We would be able to suggest to them that, in view of the representations we had made in Prague, there was no need for Germany to take any hasty action, and we should try to ascertain from the German Government what was their idea of a peaceful settlement. The answer of the German Government might be that they required what Herr Henlein had demanded in his Karlsbad speech. We might then suggest that in our view certain of these demands might be obtained, but that we regarded other demands as being unreasonable. If then the German Government refused to move from their position, His Majesty's Government could then say that they had done their best, and if, in spite of the representations they had made to the German Government, the latter nevertheless insisted on having recourse to force, they must realise what the dangers were. It must be clear to them that the French Government were bound by their treaty obligations to support Czechoslovakia, and the German Government must realise that His Majesty's Government had not said that they would also* come in, too. At this point a communication would be made to the German Government on the lines of the speech he had made in the House of Commons on the 24th March, 1938. He would like to know whether his French friends would regard the course of action he had just outlined as a possible line of approach. M. Daladier said he would like to examine this suggestion rather more closely with his colleagues of the French delegation, but at first sight it seemed to him to mark a rapprochement between the British and French views. It was clear to him that there was no difference of view as regards our general ideas and the objects we both had in mind. The differences had only arisen in regard to the means by which these objects could be achieved. These differences arose from the difference in the circumstances of the two countries.

(The meeting was then adjourned for a few minutes.)

* The word "also" is pencilled through on the copy of the text from which this document is printed. It is likely that owing to an error in transcription the word "not" has been omitted from the text.

On the resumption of the conversations, M. Bonnet said that, in order to avoid confusion, he had recapitulated in a short note his understanding of the proposals which the Prime Minister had put forward.

The conclusion reached, after some discussion, was that both Governments were agreed that there should be a *démarche* by His Majesty's Government alone in Berlin. They would explain to the German Government that they were doing their best to find a peaceful solution of the Sudeten difficulty and had asked Dr. Benes to make his contribution, but it took two to reach an agreement, and they therefore wished to know what was the position of the German Government. They wished to impress on the German Government that, in the meantime, and in view of their intervention at Prague, there was no need, nor indeed any reason, for action on the part of the German Government. Simultaneously, a *démarche* would be made at Prague by both the French and the British Governments to secure the maximum concessions from Dr. Benes. If, however, a peaceful solution were not reached by this means, His Majesty's Government would then say to the German Government that they had done everything they could; if, in spite of this, the German Government intended to resort to force, they would be doing so in full knowledge of the dangers of which they were aware, namely, that France would be compelled to intervene by virtue of her obligations, and that His Majesty's Government could not guarantee that they would not do the same. In this connexion His Majesty's Government would make use of the phrases used by Mr. Chamberlain in his speech in the House of Commons on the 24th March, 1938.

September 1938: (*Left to right*) Goering, Hitler, Dr. Schmidt (interpreter), Count Ciano (Italian Foreign Minister), Mussolini, Daladier, and Chamberlain at the Munich Conference. (AP/Wide World Photos)

PART IV Munich

Neville Chamberlain

A Quarrel in a Far-away Country

In this justly famous address, broadcast on September 27, 1938, at a time when many were convinced war would begin at any moment, Chamberlain emphasized that he had made every effort to save Britain from a war over a "quarrel in a far-away country between people of whom we know nothing." He also assured his people that he would not cease his efforts for peace. These efforts, of course, led to the Munich conference only three days later.

From Sir Arthur Bryant, ed., *In Search of Peace (1937–1938) by the Right Honourable Nevelle Chamberlain, M.P.* 1939, pp. 274–276. Published by Century Hutchinson Ltd.

To-morrow Parliament is going to meet, and I shall be making a full statement of the events which have led up to the present anxious and critical situation.

An earlier statement would not have been possible when I was flying backwards and forwards across Europe, and the position was changing from hour to hour. But to-day there is a lull for a brief time, and I want to say a few words to you, men and women of Britain and the Empire, and perhaps to others as well.

First of all I must say something to those who have written to my wife or myself in these last weeks to tell us of their gratitude for my efforts and to assure us of their prayers for my success. Most of these letters have come from women—mothers or sisters of our own countrymen. But there are countless others besides—from France, from Belgium, from Italy, even from Germany, and it has been heartbreaking to read of the growing anxiety they reveal and their intense relief when they thought, too soon, that the danger of war was past.

If I felt my responsibility heavy before, to read such letters has made it seem almost overwhelming. How horrible, fantastic, incredible it is that we should be digging trenches and trying on gas-masks here because of a quarrel in a faraway country between people of whom we know nothing. It seems still more impossible that a quarrel which has already been settled in principle should be the subject of war.

I can well understand the reasons why the Czech Government have felt unable to accept the terms which have been put before them in the German memorandum. Yet I believe after my talks with Herr Hitler that, if only time were allowed, it ought to be possible for the arrangements for transferring the territory that the Czech Government has agreed to give to Germany to be settled by agreement under conditions which would assure fair treatment to the population concerned.

You know already that I have done all that one man can do to compose this quarrel. After my visits to Germany I have realised vividly how Herr Hitler feels that he must champion other Germans, and his indignation that grievances have not been met before this. He told me privately, and last night he repeated publicly, that after this Sudeten German question is settled, that is the end of Germany's territorial claims in Europe.

After my first visit to Berchtesgaden I did get the assent of the Czech Government to proposals which gave the substance of what Herr Hitler wanted and I was taken completely by surprise when I got back to Germany and found that he insisted that the territory should be handed over to him immediately, and immediately occupied by German troops without previous arrangements for safeguarding the people within the territory who were not Germans, or did not want to join the German Reich.

I must say that I find this attitude unreasonable. If it arises out of any doubts that Herr Hitler feels about the intentions of the Czech Government to carry out their promises and hand over the territory, I have offered on the part of the British Government to guarantee their words, and I am sure the value of our promise will not be underrated anywhere.

I shall not give up the hope of a peaceful solution, or abandon my efforts for peace, as long as any chance for peace remains. I would not hesitate to pay even a third visit to Germany if I thought it would do any good. But at this moment I see nothing further that I can usefully do in the way of mediation.

Meanwhile there are certain things we can and shall do at home. Volunteers are still wanted for air raid precautions, for fire brigade and police services, and for the Territorial units. I know that all of you, men and women alike, are ready to play your part in the defence of the country, and I ask you all to offer your services, if you have not already done so, to the local authorities, who will tell you if you are wanted and in what capacity.

Do not be alarmed if you hear of men being called up to man the anti-aircraft defences or ships. These are only precautionary measures such as a Government must take in times like this. But they do not necessarily mean that we have determined on war or that war is imminent.

However much we may sympathise with a small nation confronted by a big and powerful neighbour, we cannot in all circumstances undertake to involve the whole British Empire in war simply on her account. If we have to fight it must be on larger issues than that. I am myself a man of peace to the depths of my soul. Armed conflict between nations is a nightmare to me; but if I were convinced that any nation had made up its mind to dominate the world by fear of its force, I should feel that it must be resisted. Under such a domination life for people who believe in liberty would not be worth living; but war is a fearful thing, and we must be very clear, before we embark on it, that it is really the great issues that are at stake, and that the call to risk everything in their defence, when all the consequences are weighed, is irresistible.

For the present I ask you to await as calmly as you can the events of the next few days. As long as war has not begun, there is always hope that it may be prevented, and you know that I am going to work for peace to the last moment. Good night.

Harold Nicolson

For a Second, the House Was Hushed

Harold Nicolson, diplomat, historian, Member of Parliament, and diarist, recorded the dramatic events in the House of Commons of September 28, 1938, in which Chamberlain described the efforts for peace of his government, including his dramatic flights to Germany. After an hour, a piece of paper was handed him—the invitation to Munich—and the House of Commons reacted just as did the nation soon thereafter.

28th September, 1938

I walk down to the House at 2:15 P.M. passing through Trafalgar Square and down Whitehall. The pigeons are clustering round the fountains and there is a group of children feeding them. My companion says to me, "Those children ought to be evacuated at once, and so should the pigeons." As we get near the House of Commons there is a large shuffling, shambling crowd and people putting fresh flowers at the base of the Cenotaph. The crowd is very silent and anxious. They stare at us with dumb, inquisitive eyes.

When we got into the Chamber our eyes were riveted upon a strange metal honeycomb rising in front of the Prime Minister's seat. We realised that this meant that for the first time in the history of the House of Commons, a speech was to be broadcast. This filled us with mingled horror and pride in the occasion.

The Speaker began by announcing the death of previous Members, and he had hardly finished with the obituary list before the Prime Minister entered from behind his chair. He was greeted with wild applause by his supporters, many of whom rose in their seats and waved their order-papers. The Labour Opposition, the Liberal Opposition and certain of the National supporters remained seated.

Mr. Chamberlain rose slowly in his place and spread the manuscript of his speech upon the box in front of him. The House was hushed in silent expectancy. From the Peers' Gallery above the clock the calm face of Lord Baldwin peered down upon the arena in which he himself had so often battled. Mr. Chamberlain began with a chronological statement of the events which had led up to the crisis. He spoke in calm and measured tones and the House listened to him in dead silence. The only interruption was made by the Messengers of the House who, as always happens, kept on passing along the benches the telegrams and pink telephone slips which were pouring in upon Members. Mr. Winston Churchill, who sits at the end of my own row, received so many telegrams that they were clipped together by an elastic band. Mr. Attlee sat opposite Mr. Chamberlain with his feet on the table looking like an amiable little bantam. The first burst of applause occurred when Mr. Chamberlain mentioned Lord Runciman's great services, and as he did so, he removed his pince-nez between his finger and thumb, raised his face to the skylight and spoke with friendly conviction. Being an experienced Parliamentarian, he would abandon his manuscript at moments and speak extempore.

The chronological method which he adopted increased the dramatic tension of the occasion. We all knew more or less what had happened in August and the early weeks of September, and we were waiting for his statement of what had occurred during the last few hours. He reached the point where he described the fourth plan of President Benes. The mention of this plan was received with loud cheers, and he described it in precise terms, having taken off his pince-nez and holding them between finger and thumb. "On Friday, 23rd September," he said, "a Cabinet meeting was held again. . . ." The House leant forward, realising that he was passing from that part of the story which we already knew to the part that had not yet been divulged. He went on to describe his negotiations with the Czechs and the French and to tell us how he had felt it necessary himself to visit Herr Hitler "as a last resort." When he said these words, "as a last resort," he whipped off his pince-nez and looked up at the skylight with an expression of grim hope. He then described his visit to Berchtesgaden. "It was," he said with a wry grin, "my first flight," and he described the whole visit as "this adventure." He said that his conversation with Herr Hitler had convinced him that the Führer was prepared, on behalf of the Sudeten Germans, "to risk a world war." As he said these words a shudder of horror passed through the House of Commons.

"I came back," he added, "to London the next day." The House was tense with excitement. He then told us how the Anglo-French plan was described by Hitler at Godesberg as "too dilatory." "Imagine," he said, "the perplexity in which I found myself." This remark aroused a murmur of sympathetic appreciation from all benches.

"Yesterday morning," began the Prime Minister, and we were all conscious that some revelation was approaching. He began to tell us of his final appeal to Herr Hitler and Signor Mussolini. I glanced at the clock. It was twelve minutes after four. The Prime Minister had been speaking for exactly an hour. I noticed that a sheet of Foreign Office paper was being rapidly passed along the Government bench. Sir John Simon interrupted the Prime Minister and there was a momentary hush. He adjusted his pince-nez and read the document that had been handed to him. His whole face, his whole body, seemed to change. He raised his face so that the light from the ceiling fell full upon it. All the lines of anxiety and weariness seemed suddenly to have been smoothed out; he appeared ten years younger and triumphant. "Herr Hitler," he said, "has just agreed to postpone his mobilisation for twenty-four hours and to meet me in conference with Signor Mussolini and Signor Daladier at Munich."

That, I think, was one of the most dramatic moments which I have ever witnessed. For a second, the House was hushed in absolute silence. And then the whole House burst into a roar of cheering, since they knew that this might mean peace. That was the end of the Prime Minister's speech, and when he sat down the whole House rose as a man to pay a tribute to his achievement.

. . . I find an immense sense of *physical* relief, in that I shall not be afraid tonight of the German bombs. But my moral anxieties are in no way diminished. The P.M., when he read out his final message this afternoon, had, it is true, a look of spiritual delight, but somewhere about it was the glow of personal triumph. I believe that he seriously imagines that Mussolini has made this gesture out of friendship for the Chamberlain family. He does not even now understand that what did the trick was the mobilisation of the fleet and our proclaimed alliance with France and Russia. When all his supporters crowded round him to congratulate him afterwards, he showed great satisfaction and even greater self-satisfaction. Winston came up: "I congratulate you on your good fortune. You were very lucky." The P.M. didn't like that at all.

Stuart Hodgson

The World's Debt to Neville Chamberlain

Despite the efforts of many historians, and knowing the result of the appeasement policy, contemporary readers still find it all too easy to

From *The Man Who Made the Peace: Neville Chamberlain*, 1938, pp. 139–143, E. P. Dutton.

overlook the admiration that so many Europeans—and millions of non-Europeans, for that matter—had for Chamberlain, the hero of Munich. In this excerpt from a best-selling book published immediately following the infamous meeting, British journalist Stuart Hodgson illustrates the reason for that short-lived adoration: Chamberlain was the man, it seemed, who had saved them from the horror of war.

"When I was a very little boy," said the tired voice on the microphone, as Mr. Neville Chamberlain set out from Heston on his flight to Munich, "I used to be told, 'If at first you don't succeed, try, try, try again.' That is what I am doing."

Was there ever any great occasion in history in which the main actor at the crisis of the drama expressed himself in language quite like that? It is difficult to think of any man—with the possible exception of Abraham Lincoln—who would have used words quite so simple and artless as if he were speaking to his own children at his own fireside after dinner instead of addressing a message to which all the world was eagerly listening.

But he was speaking to all the world: and he spoke in language which all the world could understand. It is possible to criticise the peace of Munich. It is very easy! It can be represented as a callous betrayal of a small nation which trusted us to the tyrannical threats of an unscrupulous neighbour state; a nation which we were bound, morally if not legally, to defend against that precise danger. It can be represented as a betrayal of British interests, a compact which buys temporary peace at the expense of aggrandising Germany and leaving us with our alliances shattered and our prestige desperately weakened to face precisely the same menace a few years or a few months hence. It may be said, and it is being said, that when he agreed to the Munich terms, Mr. Chamberlain betrayed the cause of democracy, and needlessly; for Hitler would never have fought; or if he had fought, he would have been speedily and utterly defeated.

All this, and much else, may be said and will be said; and all of it misses the main significance of the Munich agreement, the one great fact which makes it a landmark in the history not of Britain or of Germany but of the world. A few days only before the outbreak of the war of 1914 the Germany Socialist party passed a resolution condemning war. A few days later the German Socialists were marching with their fellow countrymen to Belgium; and for four grim years of misery and slaughter nothing more was heard of the German Socialists. To all appearance they might as well have passed a resolution against earthquakes.

But the miracle for which we looked in vain in 1914 came off in 1938. Why was it that Mr. Neville Chamberlain was, to his own surprise, so wildly acclaimed by the German crowds? It is simply because he made himself the mouthpiece of the horror with which millions of men and women all over the world regard the brutish deviltries of modern war. Others helped, and had their reward. President Roosevelt helped, and won the acclaim of his countrymen in so doing. M. Daladier helped, and earned the thanks of the vast majority of French men and French women. Signor Mussolini helped, and was rewarded with such a reception when he returned home from Munich as even he has never received before. Poor President Benes helped and has at least the consolation of knowing that he stands high today in the admiring regard of millions who a month ago had scarcely heard his name. But circumstances and his own courage and tenacity made one man the acknowledged spokesman of the hatred and horror with which simple men and women everywhere regard modern war.

It seems to me monstrous to talk of this worldwide feeling as a form of cowardice or an example of mass hysteria. Is it cowardice to shrink with disgust from the thought of what will and must happen in any great war today—the blinded babies, the mangled women, the great towns going up in flames, the 30,000 casualties a day which it was estimated might be expected in London alone? A German woman during the crisis rang up a friend in England. "I do this at peril of my life," she said, "but you ought to know. The blinds are drawn, and the troops are marching here in silence without a cheer." Was she a coward? Can the weeping French women who flocked about M. Daladier on his return crying, "Thank you, thank you," be properly described as hysterical? Had they not cause for thankfulness? Was the German in the crowd at Buckingham Palace who cried out, "I am a German. Shake hands with me," a coward?

The great fact is that for the first time in history the voice of the common people of all countries, as the horrible shadow of war darkened their homes, made itself heard, and decisively. A man was found to give it expression and it prevailed—prevailed even at that eleventh hour when the issue had almost passed out of the hands of the politicians and the military machines in all countries had started on their deadly course. And what has been done once may and will be done again. The people know their power now. The politicians know that it is possible to mobilise opinion for peace as well as for war; and that he who does so effectively is assured of a triumph such as no military conqueror can win, be his victories never so great.

There may be other wars and rumours of war. The shadow may darken again the homes of countless thousands of perfectly innocent people. But next time there will be the same reaction; and next time it will be easier to organise it. That knowledge is the great prize which has been won; and the man to whom the world owes it, and knows that it owes it, is Neville Chamberlain.

Winston S. Churchill

A Disaster of the First Magnitude

Winston Churchill was certainly the most significant of the critics of Chamberlain's appeasement policy. In the debate in the House of Commons over the Munich accords, October 5, 1938, he made one of his most powerful attacks on the prime minister and his entire foreign policy. Despite the hopelessness of his position in a House dominated by Chamberlain and a nation still enraptured by the hope for peace, Churchill delivered one of his finest speeches.

From *Parliamentary Debates*, 5th Series, House of Commons, Vol. 339, Cols. 359–373.

Now I come to the point, which was mentioned to me just now from some quarters of the House, about the saving of peace. No one has been a more resolute and uncompromising struggler for peace than the Prime Minister. Everyone knows that. Never has there been such intense and undaunted determination to maintain and to secure peace. That is quite true. Nevertheless, I am not quite clear why there was so much danger of Great Britain or France being involved in a war with Germany at this juncture if, in fact, they were ready all along to sacrifice Czechoslovakia. The terms which the Prime Minister brought back with him—I quite agree at the last moment; everything had got off the rails and nothing but his intervention could have saved the peace, but I am talking of the events of the summer—could easily have been agreed, I believe, through the ordinary diplomatic channels at any time during the summer. And I will say this, that I believe the Czechs, left to themselves and told they were going to get no help from the Western Powers, would have been able to make better terms than they have got—they could hardly have worse—after all this tremendous perturbation.

There never can be any absolute certainty that there will be a fight if one side is determined that it will give way completely. When one reads the Munich terms, when one sees what is happening in Czechoslovakia from hour to hour, when one is sure, I will not say of Parliamentary approval but of Parliamentary acquiescence, when the Chancellor of the Exchequer makes a speech which at any rate tries to put in a very powerful and persuasive manner the fact that, after all, it was inevitable and indeed righteous—right—when we saw all this, and everyone on this side of the House, including many Members of the Conservative Party who are supposed to be vigilant and careful guardians of the national interest, it is quite clear that nothing vitally affecting us was at stake, it seems to me that one must ask, What was all the trouble and fuss about?

The resolve was taken by the British and the French Governments. Let me say that it is very important to realise that it is by no means a question which the British Government only have had to decide. I very much admire the manner in which, in the House, all references of a recriminatory nature have been repressed, but it must be realised that this resolve did not emanate particularly from one or other of the Governments but was a resolve for which both must share in common the responsibility. When this resolve was taken and the course was followed—you may say it was wise or unwise, prudent or short-sighted—once it had been decided not to make the defence of Czechoslovakia a matter of war, then there was really no reason, if the matter had been handled during the summer in the ordinary way, to call into being all this formidable apparatus of crisis. I think that point should be considered. . . .

France and Great Britain together, especially if they had maintained a close contact with Russia, which certainly was not done, would have been able in those days in the summer, when they had the prestige, to influence many of the smaller States of Europe, and I believe they could have determined the attitude of Poland. Such a combination, prepared at a time when the German dictator was not deeply and irrevocably committed to his new adventure, would, I believe, have given strength to all those forces in Germany which resisted this departure, this new design. They were varying forces, those of a military character which declared that Germany was not ready to undertake a world war, and all that mass of moderate opinion and popular opinion which dreaded war, and some elements of which still have some influence upon the German Government. Such action would have given strength to all that intense desire for peace which the helpless German masses share with their British and French fellow men, and which, as we have been reminded, found a passionate and rarely permitted vent in the joyous manifestations with which the Prime Minister was acclaimed in Munich.

All these forces, added to the other deterrents which combinations of Powers, great and small, ready to stand firm upon the front of law and for the ordered remedy of grievances, would have formed, might well have been effective. Of course you cannot say for certain that they would. [*Interruption.*] I try to argue fairly with the House. At the same time I do not think it is fair to charge those who wished to see this course followed, and followed consistently and resolutely, with having wished for an immediate war. Between submission and immediate war there was this third alternative, which gave a hope not only of peace but of justice. It is quite true that such a policy in order to succeed demanded that Britain should declare straight out and a long time beforehand that she would, with others, join to defend Czechoslovakia against an unprovoked aggression. His Majesty's Government refused to give that guarantee when it would have saved the situation, yet in the end they gave it when it was too late, and now, for the future, they renew it when they have not the slightest power to make it good.

All is over. Silent, mournful, abandoned, broken, Czechoslovakia recedes into the darkness. She has suffered in every respect by her association with the Western democracies and with the League of Nations, of which she has always been an obedient servant. She has suffered in particular from her association with France, under whose guidance and policy she has been actuated for so long. The very measures taken by His Majesty's Government in the Anglo-French Agreement to give her the best chance possible, namely, the 50 per cent. clean cut in certain districts instead of a plebiscite, have turned to her detriment, because there is to be a plebiscite too in wide areas, and those other Powers who had claims have also come down upon the helpless victim. Those municipal elections upon whose voting the basis is taken for the 50 per cent. cut were held on issues which had nothing to do with joining Germany. When I saw Herr Henlein over here he assured me that was not the desire of his people. Positive statements were made that it was only a question of home rule, of having a position of their own in the Czechoslovakian State. No one has a right to say that the plebiscite which is to be taken in areas under Saar conditions, and the clean-cut of the 50 per cent. areas—that those two operations together amount in the slightest degree to a verdict of self-determination. It is a fraud and a farce to invoke that name.

We in this country, as in other Liberal and democratic countries, have a perfect right to exalt the principle of self-determination, but it comes ill out of the mouths of those in totalitarian States who deny even the smallest element of toleration to every section and creed within their bounds. But, however you put it, this particular block of land, this mass of human beings to be handed over, has never expressed the desire to go into the Nazi rule. I do not believe that even now—if their opinion could be asked, they would exercise such an option. . . .

I venture to think that in future the Czechoslovak State cannot be maintained as an independent entity. You will find that in a period of time which may be measured by years, but may be measured only by months, Czechoslovakia will be engulfed in the Nazi régime. Perhaps they may join it in despair or in revenge. At any rate, that story is over and told. But we cannot consider the abandonment and ruin of Czechoslovakia in the light only of what happened only last month. It is the most grievous consequence which we have yet experienced of what we have done and of what we have left undone in the last five years—five years of futile good intention, five years of eager search started for the line of least resistance, five years of uninterrupted retreat of British power, five years of neglect of our air defences. Those are the features which I stand here to declare and which marked an improvident stewardship for which Great Britain and France have dearly to pay. We have been reduced in those five years from a position of security so overwhelming and so unchallengeable that we never cared to think about it. We have been reduced from a position where the very word "war" was considered one which would be used only by persons qualifying for a lunatic asylum. We have been reduced from a position of safety and power—power to do good, power to be generous to a beaten foe, power to make terms with Germany, power to give her proper redress for her grievances, power to stop her arming if we chose, power to take any step in strength or mercy or justice which we thought right—reduced in five years from a position safe and unchallenged to where we stand now.

When I think of the fair hopes of a long peace which still lay before Europe at the beginning of 1933 when Herr Hitler first obtained power, and of all the opportunities of arresting the growth of the Nazi power which have been thrown away, when I think of the immense combinations and resources which have been neglected or squandered, I cannot believe that a parallel exists in the whole course of history. So far as this country is concerned the responsibility must rest with those who have the undisputed control of our political affairs. They neither prevented Germany from rearming, nor did they rearm ourselves in time. They quarrelled with Italy without saving Ethiopia. They exploited and discredited the vast institution of the League of Nations and they neglected to make alliances and combinations which might have repaired previous errors, and thus they left us in the hour of trial without adequate national defence or effective international security. . . .

We are in the presence of a disaster of the first magnitude which has befallen Great Britain and France. Do not let us blind ourselves to that. It must now be accepted that all the countries of Central and Eastern Europe will make the best terms they can with the triumphant Nazi Power. The system of alliances in Central Europe upon which France has relied for her safety has been swept away, and I can see no means by which it can be reconstituted. The road down the Danube Valley to the Black Sea, the resources of corn and oil, the road which leads as far as Turkey, has been opened. In fact, if not in form, it seems to me that all those countries of Middle Europe, all those Danubian countries, will, one after another, be drawn into this vast system of power politics—not only power military politics but power economic politics—radiating from Berlin, and I believe this can be achieved quite smoothly and swiftly and will not necessarily entail the firing of a single shot. . . .

I have been casting about to see how measures can be taken to protect us from this advance of the Nazi Power, and to secure those forms of life which are so dear to us. What is the sole method that is open? The sole method that is open is for us to regain our old island independence by acquiring that supremacy in the air which we were promised, that security in our air defences which we were assured we had, and thus to make ourselves an island once again. That, in all this grim outlook, shines out as the overwhelming fact. An effort at rearmament the like of which has not been seen ought to be made forthwith, and all the resources of this country and all its united strength should be bent to that task. I was very glad to see that Lord Baldwin yesterday in the House of Lords said that he would mobilise industry to-morrow. But I think it would have been much better if Lord Baldwin had said that 2-1/2 years ago, when everyone demanded a Ministry of Supply. I will venture to say to hon. Gentlemen sitting here behind the Government Bench, hon. Friends of mine, whom I thank for the patience with which they have listened to what I have to say, that they have some responsibility for all this too, because, if they had given one tithe of the cheers they have lavished upon this transaction of Czechoslovakia to the small band of Members who were endeavouring to get timely rearmament set in motion, we should not now be in the position in which we are. Hon. Gentlemen opposite, and hon. Members on the Liberal benches, are not entitled to throw these stones. I remember for two years having to face, not only the Government's deprecation, but their stern disapproval. Lord Baldwin has now given the signal, tardy though it may be; let us at least obey it.

After all, there are no secrets now about what happened in the air and in the mobilisation of our anti-aircraft defences. These matters have been, as my hon. and gallant Friend the Member for the Abbey Division said, seen by thousands of people. They can form their own opinions of the character of the statements which have been persistently made to us by Ministers on this subject. Who pretends now that there is air parity with Germany? Who pretends now that our anti-aircraft defences were adequately manned or armed? We know that the German General Staff are well informed upon these subjects, but the House of Commons has hitherto not taken seriously its duty of requiring to assure itself on these matters. The Home Secretary [Sir Samuel Hoare] said the other night that he would welcome investigation. Many things have been done which reflect the greatest credit upon the administration. But the vital matters are what we want to know about. I have asked again and again during these three years for a secret Session where these matters could be thrashed out, or for an investigation by a Select Committee of the House, or for some other method. I ask now that, when we meet again in the autumn, that should be a matter on which the Government should take the House into its confidence, because we have a right to know where we stand and what measures are being taken to secure our position.

I do not grudge our loyal, brave people, who were ready to do their duty no matter what the cost, who never flinched under the strain of last week—I do not grudge them the natural, spontaneous outbursts of joy and relief when they learned that the hard ordeal would no longer be required of them at the moment; but they should know the truth. They should know that there has been gross neglect and deficiency in our defences; they should know that we have sustained a defeat without a war, the consequences of which will travel far with us along our road; they should know that we have passed an awful milestone in our history, when the whole equilibrium of Europe has been deranged, and that the terrible words have for the time being been pronounced against the Western democracies:

> *"Thou are weighed in the balance and found wanting."*

And do not suppose that this is the end. This is only the beginning of the reckoning. This is only the first sip, the first foretaste of a bitter cup which will be proffered to us year by year unless by a supreme recovery of moral health and martial vigour, we arise again and take our stand for freedom as in the olden time.

The Munich Accords

Almost forgotten in the discussion over appeasement in general and the Munich conference in particular are the actual agreements signed by Chamberlain, Daladier, Hitler, and Mussolini on September 29, 1938. Actually drafted by the German foreign office but presented as his own by Mussolini, the agreements gave the Fuhrer virtually everything he wanted at the time—except for a swift and victorious war to crush the Czechs. Also included is the text of the brief statement Chamberlain forced on Hitler the following day. To Chamberlain it was a pledge of mutual good will; to Hitler it meant nothing. It became rather infamous after the prime minister read it aloud at Heston Airport upon his return.

The Munich Agreement

Germany, the United Kingdom, France, and Italy, taking into consideration the agreement, which had been already reached in principle for the cession to Germany of the Sudeten German territory, have agreed on the following terms and conditions governing the said cession and the measures consequent thereon, and by this agreement they each hold themselves responsible for the steps necessary to secure its fulfillment:

From *Documents on British Foreign Policy, 1919–1939*, Third Series, Vol. II, 1949, pp. 627–640. Reprinted with permission from Her Majesty's Stationery Office.

1. The evacuation will begin 1st October.
2. The United Kingdom, France and Italy agree that the evacuation of the territory shall be completed by the 10th October, without any existing installations having been destroyed and that the Czechoslovak Government will be held responsible for carrying out the evacuation without damage to the said installations.
3. The conditions governing the evacuation will be laid down in detail by an international commission composed of representatives of Germany, the United Kingdom, France, Italy and Czechoslovakia.
4. The occupation by stages of the predominantly German territory by German troops will begin on the 1st October. The four territories marked on the attached map will be occupied by German troops in the following order: the territory marked No. I on the 1st and 2nd of October, the territory marked No. II on the 2nd and 3rd of October, the territory marked No. III on the 3rd, 4th and 5th of October, the territory marked No. IV on the 6th and 7th of October. The remaining territory of preponderantly German character will be ascertained by the aforesaid international commission and will be occupied by German troops by the 10th of October.
5. The international commission referred to in paragraph 3 will determine the territories in which a plebiscite is to be held. These territories will be occupied by international bodies until the plebiscite has been completed. The same commission will fix the conditions in which the plebiscite is to be held, taking as a basis the conditions of the Saar plebiscite. The commission will also fix a date, not later than the end of November, on which the plebiscite will be held.
6. The final determination of the frontiers will be carried out by the international commission. This commission will also be entitled to recommend to the four Powers, Germany, the United Kingdom, France and Italy, in certain exceptional cases minor modifications in the strictly

ethnographical determination of the zones which are to be transferred without plebiscite.

7. There will be a right of option into and out of the transferred territories, the option to be exercised within six months from the date of this agreement. A German-Czechoslovak commission shall determine the details of the option, consider ways of facilitating the transfer of population and settle questions of principle arising out of the said transfer.
8. The Czechoslovak Government will within a period of four weeks from the date of this agreement release from their military and police forces any Sudeten Germans who may wish to be released, and the Czechoslovak Government will within the same period release Sudeten German prisoners who are serving terms of imprisonment for political offences.

Adolf Hitler
Neville Chamberlain
Edouard Daladier
Benito Mussolini

Munich
September 29, 1938

Annex to the Agreement

His Majesty's Government of the United Kingdom and the French Government have entered into the above agreement on the basis that they stand by the offer, contained in paragraph 6 of the Anglo-French proposals of the 19th September, relating to an international guarantee of the new boundaries of the Czechoslovak State against unprovoked aggression.

Adolf Hitler
Neville Chamberlain
Edouard Daladier
Benito Mussolini

Munich
September 29, 1938

Declaration

The Heads of the Governments of the four Powers declare that the problems of the Polish and Hungarian minorities in Czechoslovakia, if not settled within three months by agreement between the respective Governments, shall form the subject of another meeting of the Heads of the Governments of the four Powers here present.

Adolf Hitler
Neville Chamberlain
Edouard Daladier
Benito Mussolini

Munich
September 29, 1938

Supplementary Declaration

All questions which may arise out of the transfer of the territory shall be considered as coming within the terms of reference to the international commission.

Adolf Hitler
Neville Chamberlain
Edouard Daladier
Benito Mussolini

Munich
September 29, 1938

Composition of the International Commission

The four Heads of Government here present agree that the international commission provided for in the agreement signed by them to-day shall consist of the secretary of State in the German Foreign Office, the British, French and Italian ambassadors accredited in Berlin, and a representative to be nominated by the Government of Czechoslovakia.

Adolf Hitler
Neville Chamberlain
Edouard Daladier
Benito Mussolini

Munich
September 29, 1938

The Supplementary Agreement Between Neville Chamberlain and Adolf Hitler

We regard the agreement signed last night and the Anglo-German Naval Agreement as symbolic of the desire of our two peoples never to go to war with one another again.

We are resolved that the method of consultation shall be the method adopted to deal with any other questions that may concern our two countries, and we are determined to continue our efforts to remove possible sources of differences and thus to contribute to assuring the peace of Europe.

Neville Chamberlain
Adolf Hitler

30 September 1938

March 1939: Elation, tears, and shock greet German troops during the occupation of Prague, in violation of the Munich agreements. (Interfoto Pressebild Agentur)

PART

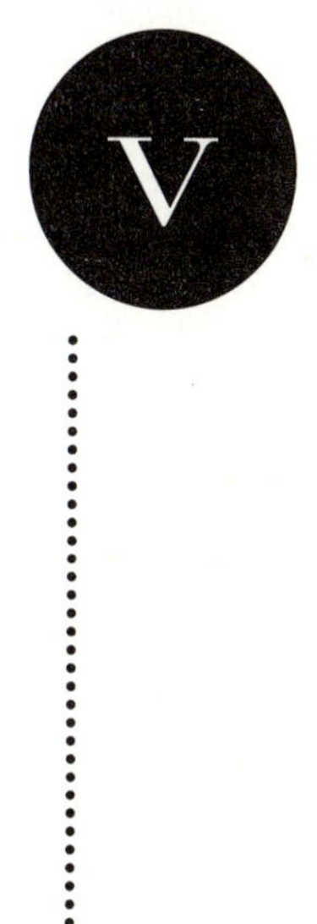

The Change of Course

Telford Taylor

The Guarantee to Poland—and After

On March 15, 1939, only six months after signing the Munich accords, Hitler seized control of the rest of Czechoslovakia. In the following selection, Telford Taylor outlines the change of direction in British policy that followed. In late March, due in part to the rumor (brought from Germany by journalist Ian Colvin) that Hitler meant to launch an immediate attack to the east, Britain declared a guarantee of Poland. There followed further guarantees to small nations, a futile attempt to

From *Munich: The Price of Peace*, 1979, pp. 966–977. New York: Vintage/Random House.

reach agreement with the Soviet Union over the formation of an anti-Hitler bloc, and, ultimately, the declaration of war and the final admission of the failure of appeasement.

The bearer of alarming tidings this time was Ian Colvin, Berlin correspondent of the London *News Chronicle*. In January, Colvin had been told by "a reliable source" that "a victualling contractor to the German army had then received instructions to provide the same amount of rations as he had supplied in September 1938, and to have them ready by March 28th, 1939," for delivery "in an area of Pomerania that formed a rough wedge pointing to the railway junction of Bromberg in the Polish corridor." On March 27 the German press carried reports of anti-German excesses in Bromberg, which Colvin thought resembled the charges against the Czechs in the Sudetenland prior to Munich. He put all this to Mason-Mac, who "agreed that a rapid move to cut the Polish corridor might be intended, though he had no positive information," and advised Colvin to take the information to London in person.

Colvin flew to London on the twenty-eighth, and through Sir Reginald Leeper (head of the Foreign Office News Department) arranged to see Cadogan, Simon, and Halifax on the twenty-ninth. Late that afternoon Halifax took Colvin to Downing Street, and Colvin told his story to the Prime Minister in the presence of Halifax, Cadogan, Leeper, and Dunglass. Harvey was told that Colvin made a "great impression," and that must have been the case, for Cadogan recorded that Halifax remained with Chamberlain after the meeting and then came to the Foreign Office with the information that the Prime Minister had "agreed to the idea of an *immediate* declaration in support of Poland, to counter a quick putsch by Hitler." Halifax, Butler, Cadogan, and others stayed until the small hours in the morning of the thirtieth, drafting the declaration and the dispatches to Paris and Warsaw which its issuance would entail.

A special Cabinet meeting was called the next morning to consider these documents and the new situation to which they were addressed. Halifax explained that the reason for the meeting was that "information received on the previous day appeared to disclose a possible German intention to execute a *coup de main* against Poland," and summarized what Colvin had reported. The proposal he wished the Cabinet to consider was "that we should make a clear declaration of our intention to support Poland if Poland was attacked by Germany," primarily for the purpose of deterring Hitler from taking such action.

Carefully Halifax listed objections to such a commitment: it would give [Polish Foreign Minister Josef] Beck "what he wanted without obtaining any reciprocal undertaking from him"; it might upset the prospects of direct agreement between Germany and Poland; it might provoke Germany to take the very action that was sought to be prevented; it was drastic action to take "on the meagre information available to us." For all these reasons, Halifax did not propose to issue the declaration at once, but to have its text approved by the Cabinet, the leaders of the Opposition, and the French, so that it could "be published at a moment's notice, if the situation should require it."

The Prime Minister, acknowledging that "the action now proposed was a serious step and was the actual crossing of the stream," supported the proposal:

> *It had already been pointed out, as a result of the German action against Czechoslovakia, instead of the Czech army being on our side, Czech resources were now available to Germany. It would be a very serious matter if Poland, instead of being a potential ally, also became added to the resources of Germany. If, therefore, we took no action, there was a risk that, in a short time, we should find that Poland had been over-run and that we had missed an opportunity. On the other hand, if we uttered a warning such as was now proposed, we should be commited to intervention if Germany persisted in aggression.*

There followed a long discussion, in which Chatfield took the leading part. Referring to a report submitted by the Chiefs of Staff, he declared that they had come "to a fairly definite conclusion that, if we have to fight Germany, it would be better to do so with Poland as an ally, rather than to allow Poland to be absorbed and dominated by Germany without making any effort to help her." Even though Poland might be overrun, Germany would suffer heavy casualties and the Germans would have to leave considerable forces there. On the other hand, the Chiefs had "no evidence that either the Germans or the Italians intend to make any major move," and doubted that an attack on the Polish Corridor was imminent, though something might be planned for Danzig.

No one directly opposed the plan, though Kingsley Wood and Lord Zetland expressed grave doubts. But the language of the draft statement and telegrams caused prolonged discussion, in the course of which Chatfield pointed out a flaw in Halifax's proposed timing: if they waited for further information, the attack might occur before the statement had been issued, in which case it would be useless as a deterrent. He proposed instead the prompt issuance of a "more general statement . . . which would give more timely warning," and this was agreed to, with the further suggestion that the statement be handled by a parliamentary question-and-answer on the thirty-first. In conclusion, the Foreign Policy Committee was authorized to draft the statement and send the telegrams to Warsaw and Paris.

The draft was settled, and both Warsaw and Paris promptly agreed to the procedure. Opposition leaders were "much disturbed" at the evident exclusion of Russia from the new arrangement, and not wholly mollified by the Prime Minister's assurance that "the absence of any reference to Russia . . . was based on expediency and not on any ideological ground." British intelligence had uncovered nothing that confirmed the likelihood of a German military move, and the question to be asked and answered in Parliament was modified: "To ask the Prime Minister whether he could make any statement on the European situation." The Cabinet approved the whole procedure, and that afternoon, March 31, 1939, Neville Chamberlain answered the question:

> *. . . His Majesty's Government have no official confirmation of the rumours of any projected attack on Poland and they must not, therefore, be taken as true. . . .*
>
> *As the House is aware, certain consultations are now proceeding with other Governments. In order to make perfectly clear the position of His Majesty's Government in the meantime before these consultations are concluded, I now have to inform the House that during that period, in the event of any action which clearly threatened Polish independence, and which the Polish Government accord-*

> *ingly considered it vital to resist with their national forces, His Majesty's Government would feel themselves bound at once to lend the Polish Government all support in their power. They have given the Polish Government an assurance to this effect.*
>
> *I may add that the French Government have authorized me to make it plain that they stand on the same position in this matter as do His Majesty's Government.*

The British had crossed the Rubicon. It would be too much to say that Ian Colvin built the bridge, for in all probability a comparable commitment to Poland would have been made following Beck's visit. But the timing, setting, and unilateral character of the guarantee were, indeed, the product of Colvin's story, even though by the time Chamberlain announced the undertaking, the journalist's warning had lost much of its force.

Colvin's appearance at the Foreign Office coincided with . . . [the deterioration of German-Polish relations] and with Hitler's first thoughts about military steps against Poland. Of these things Colvin knew nothing, and his real contribution was that he got the British ministers thinking primarily in terms of Poland rather than Rumania, which was a much more accurate assessment of the direction of Hitler's next move. But at the time there was as yet no German plan for an attack against Poland, much less any deployment of forces with which to carry it out.

Hitler returned from Memel to Berlin on March 24 and went to Munich the following day. Before leaving Berlin he gave information and instructions to Brauchitsch on many aspects of the international situation, recorded in a memorandum by the general's adjutant, Major Siewert. With regard to Poland, he wrote:

> *The Führer does not wish . . . to solve the Danzig problem forcefully. He does not wish thus to drive Poland into England's arms. . . . For the time being, the Führer does not intend to solve the Polish question. However, it should now be worked on. A solution in the near future would have to be based on especially favorable political conditions. In that case Poland shall be knocked out so completely that it will not be a political factor for the next decades. . . .*

This was minatory but not immediate. The "work" on the "Polish problem" was commenced early in April, pursuant to a directive to the Wehrmacht signed by Hitler on the eleventh, which gave the cover name "Case White" to a plan "to destroy the Polish armed forces." It specified September 1, 1939, as the date by which preparations were to be completed, and that proved to be the day the Second World War began.

Neither Colvin nor the British Government had any knowledge of these directives and plans. In default of sure information on Hitler's intentions, London had to do the best it could with reports such as Colvin's and, given the tension of the times, it is not surprising that the Government thought it prudent to act on the basis that the pictured dangers were real.

Far more important and difficult to appraise is the rapidity with which the British Government reversed its basic European policy. In September, Chamberlain had exercised every means to make it possible for the French to avoid fulfillment of their guarantee to Czechoslovakia. Six months later, he and Halifax, without any request from Warsaw or Paris, breathed new life into the Franco-Polish alliance and themselves assumed parallel obligations. What accounted for this 180-degree turn? And why was it so readily followed by their Cabinet colleagues and the Parliament?

Some weeks later (May 22) Cadogan summarized the reasons as he saw them:

> *The principal object of our guarantee to Poland was to deter Germany from any further acts of aggression, and by obtaining a reciprocal guarantee from Poland to ensure that, if war came, Germany would have to fight on two fronts. . . . Germany is unable at the moment to embark on a war on two fronts. If she were free to expand eastward and to obtain control of the resources of Central and Eastern Europe, she might then be strong enough to turn upon the Western countries with overwhelming strength.*

Halifax, in his memoirs, said much the same. If it was Hitler's intention to dominate Europe:

> *. . . it might still be possible to deter him from its execution if, as we had failed to do in 1914, we made it unmistakably clear that the particular acts of aggression which he was believed to have in mind would result in a general war. And if . . . Hitler was not to be restrained, it was better that the nations under threat should stand and fight together than that they should await German attack one by one. That was in two sentences the justification for the decision to give guarantees.*

Chamberlain's and Chatfield's comments in Cabinet . . . were to the same general effect. It all amounted to the double proposition that the certain prospect of a general war might deter Hitler and keep the peace and, if not, Britain and France would have allies in the east who would involve Germany in a two-front war.

That was very well as far as it went, but all these reasons were operative in 1938 and were disregarded. Indeed, they were then even stronger, for Czechoslovakia was a much more desirable eastern ally than Poland. The Czechs had fewer divisions, but they were better armed, the country had natural defenses, extensive fortifications, and a strong armaments industry, and Russia was her ally instead of, as the Poles viewed her, an enemy.

Halifax, again in his memoirs, explained that after the events of March 15th "it was no longer possible to hope that Hitler's purposes and ambitions were limited by any boundaries of race, and the lust of continental or world mastery seemed to stand out in stark relief. Here indeed was the simple explanation a few weeks later of the guarantee given to Poland." That amounts to saying that, if the British leaders had known in September 1938 what they learned in March 1939, they would have acted otherwise on the earlier date—in other words, that they acted wrongly in 1938 because of insufficient information.

All in all, this comes fairly close to the mark. Essentially, it was a case of "once bitten, twice shy." The records do not show that any of the British ministers or top civil servants invoked the name of Eyre Crowe or quoted his famous memorandum of 1907 on the "balance of power," but they were following his teaching. In these terms, the rebirth of German military power, *provided it did not go too far*, was a harmless and even desirable counterweight to French dominance of the Europe of Versailles. In the mid-thirties it became apparent that the German development might well go too far, but Britain and France lacked the will to cut her back by force. In 1938 the gravity of the German peril became apparent, but their own weakness led most of the British leaders to look for reasons to avoid a military confrontation; Chamberlain found them in a belief that Hitler would observe the limits which he himself had announced, and the Chiefs of Staff on the ground that delay would work to Britain's military advantage. The destruction of Czechoslovakia on March 15 convinced Chamberlain and the public that Hitler would not observe those limits, and the Chiefs of Staff that a delay which enabled him to extend his sway over more of Central and Eastern Europe would work to Britain's military disadvantage.

This analysis led to the conclusion that any further German move should be met by force, but not necessarily to a guarantee of support for Poland. The announced purpose of the guarantee was deterrence, and it failed. Another purpose, less openly acknowledged, was to encourage the Poles to refuse any German demands which would seriously weaken them, and to resist an attack. The Poles did so, but very probably would have fought even had there been no guarantee. From the British standpoint, its main value was internal and psychological. From then on everyone knew or assumed that war between Germany and Poland meant war between Britain and Germany. This was a useful stimulant to rearmament, though the pace remained far below a war tempo.

The wisdom of the guarantee to Poland has been much criticized. Liddell Hart, for example, called it "foolish, futile, and provocative" and "an ill-considered gesture." But the gist of his complaint was not so much that Poland had been guaranteed as that Russia had been excluded, and that remains, in retrospect, the vital flaw in British policy at the time.

The Chiefs of Staff were sound in their endeavor to commit Germany to a two-front war, but obviously an alliance with Rumania or Lithuania would not accomplish that in any meaningful way. Poland was at best marginal, and the Chiefs of Staff badly overestimated her staying capacity against the Wehrmacht. Furthermore, she would probably fight anyhow, and the alliance with her was an obstacle to enlisting the Russians. But as the Prime Minister told the Cabinet on April 4, he had "very considerable distrust of Russia, and no confidence that we should obtain active and constant support from that country," and therefore "Poland was the key to the situation, and an alliance with Poland would ensure that Germany would be engaged in a war on two fronts."

Right or wrong, the guarantee to Poland was generally approved by the leading political figures, although Lloyd George voiced the doubts entertained by Liddell Hart. For the Labour Party, Arthur Greenwood congratulated Chamberlain on his "momentous" move, which would "give pause to those who sought to impose their will on others by show of the mailed fist." The Liberal leader, Sir Archibald Sinclair, echoed those sentiments, and Winston Churchill, while urging the desirability of Russian support, expressed "the most complete agreement with the Prime Minister on the matter" and declared that the guarantee gave "the most solid reassurances of peace."

After March 31 the road to war was downhill all the way. Colonel Beck proved a very tough negotiator; he readily agreed to reciprocate Britain's guarantee but would not join the British in guaranteeing Rumania or western countries such as Belgium and Holland, nor would he express any interest even in buying weaponry from the Soviet Union. The communiqué issued upon Beck's departure from London on April 6 recited that the two countries were "prepared to enter into an agreement of a permanent and reciprocal character" to replace the oral understanding, but no formal treaty was signed until late August, on the eve of war. The same day, in Berlin, Weizsaecker summoned Lipski and told him that "the most recent trend of Polish policy was altogether incomprehensible . . . we had suddenly heard strange sabre-rattling in Warsaw." The Fuehrer's "offer to Poland" (to guarantee the Polish-German borders in return for a German extraterritorial road and rail connection with East Prussia and the annexation of Danzig) "was one which would not be repeated," and "the future would show whether Poland had been well-advised in her attitude."

The next day, Good Friday, April 7, Italian troops invaded and overran Albania, adding another jewel to the rather shabby collection in Victor Emmanuel's crown. It was a flagrant violation of the provisions of the Anglo-Italian Agreement respecting maintenance of the territorial *status quo* in the Mediterranean area, and Cadogan at once concluded "that this proves Musso a gangster as Czechs proved Hitler." The Prime Minister, still clinging to his hopes for Mussolini, saw the matter otherwise. According to R. A. Butler's account:

> *On the Good Friday of 1939, which Mussolini chose for invasion of Albania, I hurried up from the country and at once called at*

No. 10 for instructions. I was led into a small room upstairs, overlooking a garden, which the Prime Minister used as a study. The window was partly open, showing a table for birdfood suspended outside. Neville seemed irritated at my intrusion and expressed surprise that I was perturbed. He said, "I feel sure Mussolini has not decided to go against us." When I started to talk about the general threat to the Balkans, he dismissed me with the words, "Don't be silly. Go home to bed," and continued to feed the birds. . . .

In line with this "cool" attitude, Chamberlain refrained from any such criticism as he had leveled against Hitler at Birmingham, and Italy was not formally charged with violating the Anglo-Italian treaty. But Albania, and subsequent reports (unfounded) that the Italians were about to attack the Greek island of Corfu, put the guarantee machinery again in operation, this time with Greece and Turkey as the intended beneficiaries.

In the case of Greece, the primary purpose was to warn Mussolini that an attack on that country would involve him in war with Britain and France. The Turkish situation was more complex. There was no sign that she was imminently threatened by either Germany or Italy, but Turkey was militarily strong and would be a valuable ally not only in the Mediterranean, but also as the guardian of access through the Dardanelles to the Black Sea coasts of Russia, Rumania, and Bulgaria.

The Turkish Government was friendly but indicated that they did not want a guarantee and preferred a less formal declaration of common purpose. The Greeks accepted with gratitude, and on April 11 the British Foreign Policy Committee approved the text of the announcement which Chamberlain would make in Parliament on the thirteenth.

However, on the tenth Tilea, accompanied by the Secretary-General of the Rumanian Foreign Ministry, M. Cretzianu, called on Halifax and Cadogan, pressing their government's request for an immediate, unilateral guarantee. They got little encouragement, as Halifax wished to maintain the pressure on Warsaw to join in guaranteeing Rumania. But on the twelfth Corbin came to Cadogan with the draft of the statement that the Quai d'Orsay proposed to issue, embodying guarantees to both Greece and Rumania. It was plainly desirable that the British and French statements should be of like scope, and Daladier was strongly of the opinion that guarantees to Poland and Greece would raise the implication that Rumania would be left to shift for herself, and invite attack by Germany or Hungary. For once, the British found the French arguments compelling, and on the thirteenth both governments announced their respective unilateral guarantees to Greece and Rumania, for the purpose of avoiding "disturbance by force or threats of force of the *status quo* in the Mediterranean and the Balkan Peninsula."

While handing out the guarantees, the British Government had taken several other steps, which were, probably, even less to Adolf Hitler's liking. When Bonnet was in London in March, Chamberlain had read him a stiff lecture on the shortcomings of the French air arm. Bonnet took it politely, but the next day riposted by urging upon Halifax the necessity of Britain's adopting military service conscription. Because of the Labour Party's intransigent opposition, this was regarded in government circles as "politically impossible." But the pressure was increasing for some move that would show that Britain "meant business," and on March 29, accepting Hore-Belisha's spur-of-the-moment suggestion, Chamberlain announced in the Commons that the Territorial Army would be doubled in size.

Albania gave rearmament another push, and Hore-Belisha spoke out publicly for both conscription and the establishment of a Ministry of Supply. On April 20 (Hitler's birthday) the Prime Minister finally yielded, and announced in the Commons that a Ministry of Supply would be established, and headed by Leslie Burgin, the then Minister of Transport—a selection which, like Inskip's, was not acclaimed. On the same day Chamberlain agreed to conscription and, after tense discussions with the union leaders, on April 26 he announced in Commons the introduction of legislation for compulsory military service for all men between the ages of twenty and twenty-one.

Two days later, in the course of a long address to the Reichstag, Hitler gave answer to these developments, with harsh words and news for the two principal offenders, Britain and Poland. The former was now carrying out "the policy of encirclement" and thereby "the basis for the [Anglo-German] naval treaty has been removed." A formal note denouncing the treaty was on its way to the British Government. As for Poland, the mutual Anglo-Polish guarantees were "contradictory to the agreement which I made with Marshal Pilsudski." Accordingly a memorandum had been sent to the Polish Government denouncing the nonaggression declaration of 1934.

Secret military preparations for the attack against Poland were already under way when Hitler spoke. During May the leading staff officers were drawing tactical plans, and on the twenty-third Hitler called a meeting of the service commanders-in-chief and their chiefs of staff, together with Keitel, Warlimont, and the OKW adjutants, to "indoctrinate" them politically, announce his decision "to attack Poland at the first suitable opportunity," and warn them that there would be "no repetition of the Czech affair" and "there will be war."

Meanwhile Mussolini, whose nose had been put out of joint by the German occupation of Bohemia and Moravia, had been recovering from his pique with the help of the Albanian conquest, pallid as it was. Japan was still holding back from the Tripartite Pact project, and early in May, while Ribbentrop and Ciano were conferring in Milan, the Duce suddenly decided that an alliance between the two Axis countries should be signed promptly. Hitler gave his approval, and on May 7, at the conclusion of the Ribbentrop-Ciano meeting, the communiqué announced that it had been "decided finally to define, in a formal manner, the relations between the two States of the Axis in a political and military pact." The resulting "Treaty of Friendship and Alliance" (commonly known as the "Pact of Steel") was signed by Ribbentrop and Ciano in Berlin on May 22. Its principal provision bound each of the contracting parties, in the event that the other became "involved in hostilities with another Power or Powers," to "come immediately to its side as ally and support it with all its military forces on land, sea, and in the air."

The Pact of Steel wrote finis to Chamberlain's efforts to weaken the Italo-German relation, but it came as no surprise, and the British leaders were busy with other diplomatic problems, of which the largest, by far, was what to do about Soviet Russia. On April 18 in Moscow, Litvinov handed to the British Ambassador, Sir William Seeds, an official proposal for an Anglo-Franco-Russian alliance binding the three countries to "render mutually all manner of assistance, including that of a military nature, in case of aggression in Europe" against any one of them, or against "Eastern European States situated between the Baltic and Black Seas and Bordering on U.S.S.R.," and not to negotiate or conclude peace "with aggressors separately from one another and without common consent of the three Powers."

This was a real blockbuster, full of domestic political as well as diplomatic and military problems. It was considered the following day by the Foreign Policy Committee, with the benefit of a memorandum by Cadogan, which described the Soviet proposal as "extremely inconvenient," minimized the help which Russia could give, listed several objections to the plan and declared that "from the practical point of view, there was every argument against accepting the Russian proposal." But then it was observed that "there is great difficulty in rejecting the Soviet offer," because "the left in this country may be counted on" to exploit a rejection, and there was a "very remote" risk that the result might be to turn Moscow toward an agreement with Berlin. However, the memorandum concluded that "on balance" the Soviet offers should be rejected as likely to "alienate our friends and reinforce the propaganda of our enemies without bringing in exchange any real material contribution to the strength of our Front."

Cadogan's advice was congenial to the Prime Minister (Halifax was absent) and most of the committee members. Only Hoare and Chatfield were at all receptive to the Soviet project, and the former successfully insisted that the Chiefs of Staff furnish a report on "the military value of Russian assistance" before any decision was reached. In the meantime, the French (who had also received the proposal) were to be asked not to reply until there had been consultation, and the whole matter was to be held secret.

For the Chamberlain government, the situation was indeed "very awkward." An outright rejection of the Soviet proposal, once it became known, would call down upon them the wrath not only of the Labour and Liberal opposition, but also of Churchill, Eden, and the other Conservative dissidents. It soon became apparent that the French were favorably disposed toward using the Soviet plan, at least as the basis for further discussion. But the Polish and

Rumanian objections reinforced the intense dislike and distrust of Moscow which Chamberlain, Halifax, Simon, Inskip, Wilson, Cadogan and others shared, and which no doubt helped to inflate their notions of Poland's importance and durability as keystone of the second front.

The Chiefs of Staff report on April 24 was a reasonably objective summary of the Russian military pluses and minuses, but its conclusion played into Chamberlain's hands by declaring, no doubt accurately, that "the positive assistance, whether it be in the shape of military support, or of supplying war material, which Russia could afford to Roumania, Poland, or Turkey is not so great as might be supposed generally." This rather submerged the following observation that "Russian cooperation would be invaluable in that Germany would be unable to draw upon Russia's immense reserves of food and raw materials and should succumb more quickly to our economic stranglehold."

The following day the Foreign Policy Committee, in a brief meeting, unanimously agreed not to accept either the Soviet proposal or a proposed French counterproposal. But how to put the matter to Moscow remained a difficult question. On the twenty-ninth Halifax was obliged to apologize to Ambassador Maisky for the delay in replying to the Soviet proposal, and before the problem was resolved, on May 3, Litvinov was relieved as Commissar for Foreign Affairs by Vyacheslav Molotov.

To anxious inquiries, both Molotov and Maisky assured the British that the change of face involved no change of policy, and that the Soviet proposals of April 18 were still in effect. But the replacement of the cosmopolitan Litvinov by the brusque, stubborn Molotov, who spoke only Russian, certainly brought a change of atmosphere, as Seeds discovered when he finally, on May 8, submitted the British reply, rejecting the alliance as incompatible with Poland's attitude and renewing the "suggestion" that Moscow issue a unilateral statement promising assistance in the event that France and Britain became "involved in hostilities" in support of their guarantee obligations.

So began a process of proposal and counterproposal which was to last for over three months, well into August. By May 22, when Halifax and Maisky conferred in Geneva, it became clear to the

British that the Soviet Government would not accept the "suggested" unilateral pronouncement. Meanwhile the Chiefs of Staff had reconsidered the problem and on May 16 advised Chatfield that: "A full-blown guarantee of mutual assistance between Great Britain and France and the Soviet Union offers certain advantages. It would present a solid front of formidable proportions against aggression. . . . If we fail to achieve any agreement with the Soviet, it might be regarded as a diplomatic defeat which would have serious military repercussion, in that it would have the immediate effect of encouraging Germany to further acts of aggression and of ultimately throwing the U.S.S.R. into her arms. . . . Furthermore, if Russia remained neutral, it would leave her in a dominating position at the end of hostilities."

Chamberlain, according to Cadogan, was "annoyed" at the Chiefs and in the Foreign Policy Committee argued against their conclusions, eliciting from Chatfield the response that the Chiefs were "very anxious that Russia should not under any circumstances become allied with Germany. Such an eventuality would create a most dangerous situation for us." Four days later, the Prime Minister was threatening privately to "resign rather than sign an alliance with the Soviet." But Halifax and Cadogan were beginning to change their minds, and by May 23, Chamberlain had yielded, most reluctantly, to proceed with negotiations on the basis of an Anglo-Franco-Soviet alliance.

And negotiate they did, with much acrimony on each side. As Cadogan viewed the process: "The Russians are impossible. We give them all they want, with both hands, and they merely slap them. Molotov is an ignorant and suspicious peasant." Ambassador Maisky, *per contra*, remained convinced that Chamberlain, dominated by the "Cliveden set," wanted the negotiations to fail and kept them going only to quiet the political opposition.

In any event, the British and French were too slow and too late. Since mid-April, German and Soviet diplomats had been probing occasionally, cautiously, and suspiciously to see whether there was any possibility of an advantageous *rapprochement* between the two countries, despite the propaganda war they had been waging since Hitler took power. At the end of May, Berlin decided to take the initiative in establishing closer contact, the first fruits of which were not gathered until mid-July, when long-suspended trade negotiations between the two countries were resumed. By August 3, Ambassador von der Schulenburg, after a meeting with Molotov, was able to inform Berlin that the Soviet Government was "increasingly prepared for improvement in German-Soviet relations, although the old mistrust of Germany persists." Ten days later Molotov sent word that the Soviet Government was "interested in a discussion" of several subjects, including a trade agreement and "the Polish question," and would like it to be held in Moscow.

From this point on, things moved very rapidly. Ribbentrop replied the same day (August 14) that he himself was prepared to make a "short visit to Moscow in order, in the name of the Führer, to set forth the Führer's views to Herr Stalin." Molotov reacted favorably, especially to the idea of a nonaggression pact, but observed that a visit by Ribbentrop would require "adequate preparation." On the nineteenth, Molotov agreed to receive Ribbentrop on August 26 or 27, but this was not soon enough for Hitler's purposes, as the attack against Poland was scheduled for the last week of August. The Fuehrer himself now took a hand in the negotiations and on August 20 sent a personal message to Stalin asking that Ribbentrop be received on the twenty-second or "at the latest" on the twenty-third, and Stalin promptly agreed to the later date.

The Treaty of Non-Aggression was signed by Molotov and Ribbentrop, in the presence of Stalin, on August 23, 1939. It contained a provision that, if either country should "become the object of belligerent action by a third party," the other country "shall in no manner lend its support to this third power"—thus ruling out any Russian aid to Britain or France if they went to war with Germany in fulfillment of their guarantees. There was also a secret protocol establishing Russia's and Germany's "respective spheres of influence in Eastern Europe," which provided the basis for the division of Poland between Germany and Russia a month later.

On August 25, the formal treaties between Poland and Britain and France were finally signed, and the news caused Hitler to postpone the attack for a few days in the hope of buying off the British with new promises. The effort failed, and early in the morning of September 1, 1939, German troops crossed the Polish border at all points of attack. Two days later Britain and France honored their guarantees and declared war against Germany.

And so, eleven months after Munich and five after the Anglo-French guarantees of Poland, "peace for our time" ran out.

February 1939: Churchill and Chamberlain, the former antagonists, as cabinet colleagues early in World War II. (AP/World Wide Photos)

PART

Assessing Appeasement: The Question of Responsibility

Sidney Aster

Chamberlain: The Guiltiest Man?

In considering the bitter attack on Chamberlain, *Guilty Men* (written by the journalists Michael Foot, Frank Owen, and Peter Howard and pseudonymously published in 1940 under the name "Cato"), Sidney Aster of the University of Toronto argues that the defenses commonly offered for Chamberlain and appeasement—isolationist public opinion, lack of dependable allies, a reticent military high command, and so on—

had in fact little effect on the prime minister's decision making. Further, he concludes, the appeasers were for all intents and purposes guilty as charged.

In defence of the Munich agreement, several arguments have proven most enduring. British public opinion was isolationist and would not have condoned a war in defence of Czechoslovakia. Certainly Chamberlain had no enthusiasm for getting involved in what he myopically described as "a quarrel in a far-away country between people of whom we know nothing." Dominion opinion, as relayed by the High Commissioners in London, pressed consistently for a peaceful resolution. War might have divided the empire, and in September 1938 Britain had no reliable allies. The problem was further compounded by the nightmare of a three front war. In November 1935 the chiefs of staffs had warned that Britain was dangerously over-extended, without the resources to defend its empire against simultaneous threats. The warning was repeated in 1938: "War against Japan, Germany and Italy simultaneously in 1938 is a commitment which neither the present nor the projected strength of our defence forces is designed to meet, even if we were in alliance with France and Russia." It has also been argued that the strongest defence of the Munich agreement was the parlous state of British rearmament. Munich bought Britain an additional year in which to accelerate the rearmament programme.

Unfortunately, none of these considerations counted for much in Chamberlain's mind at the time. His approach to foreign policy had been elaborated before he became Prime Minister. Munich was its logical culmination. War had been averted, and what he termed "a stable future for Czecho-Slovakia [*sic*] and the sterilisation of another danger spot" had been achieved. Moreover, the Munich accords were designed to insure the self-determination of three and a half million Sudeten Germans, a principle which they had been denied in the peace settlement in 1919. The demand for its application in September 1938 was the strength of Hitler's case. To have ignored it would have meant war against a cause which no western statesman could oppose. Besides, as Chamberlain had confided on 19 September to his sister, Ida, "on principle I didn't care two hoots whether the Sudetens were in the Reich or out of it according to their own wishes." That still left a question mark over the morality of this act. Peace in Europe may have been secured in the short term, as "Cato" contended, or the long term as Chamberlain hoped, but this was pacification which was bought at the expense of a third nation. For that reason alone there can be no defence of the Munich agreement.

Equally, there can be no defence based on the contention that Chamberlain was never "taken in" by Hitler. "Cato" made the case that Chamberlain "was convinced that Hitler meant to play ball. He felt sure that the German *Führer* would never go to war against Britain now." Support for these allegations derived from Chamberlain's comments on the Munich agreement as well as his views on rearmament. On his return from Munich he had stated that the Anglo-German declaration signed by himself and Hitler was "only a prelude to a larger settlement in which all Europe may find peace." From 10 Downing Street he spoke to cheering crowds of "peace with honour" and "peace for our time." He later told Parliament that "when I signed the document I meant what was in the document. I am convinced that *Herr* Hitler meant it too when he signed it." In his private papers he observed, "I got the impression that here was a man who could be relied upon when he had given his word." And in conversation with a former member of his cabinet, Chamberlain expostulated, "but I have made peace." In the Commons Chamberlain ascribed such comments to euphoria and fatigue. Yet he repeated in the same breath: "I do indeed believe that we may yet secure peace for our time."

Apologists for Munich have argued that British defence weaknesses and the need to buy time for the rearmament programme dictated foreign policy. Unfortunately, nowhere in Chamberlain's public utterances nor in his private correspondence is there a shred of supporting evidence. Time was certainly a crucial factor for the Prime Minister, but what he had in mind was the time needed to avoid war, or that Hitler would conveniently die and thus peace would be secured. Keith Feiling, the first biographer to study Chamberlain's private papers—and his most perspicacious—observed: "to gain time to arm against an inevitable war . . . was never his first motive, which was plain enough, simply the rightness of peace and the wrongness of war." Horace Wilson, Chamberlain's confidant and "Cato's" *bête noire,* likewise commented that "our policy was never designed just to postpone war, or enable us to enter war more united. The aim of appeasement was to avoid war altogether, for all time." If this is kept in mind the issue of rearmament in the post-Munich period becomes understandable.

The September crisis provided its own focus for "Cato's" invective. The cession of the Sudetenland to Germany was described as having "been crammed down the reluctant gullet of the Czech rulers and eventually, with many a groan and retch, swallowed into their stomachs." In the post-Munich parliamentary debate, "MPs vied with each other," according to "Cato," "in their exertions to lick the hand of the Premier." On one question only was unanimity achieved. The entire House was "soothed and silenced by the expressed resolve of the Government now to set about the rearmament of Britain with energy." Chamberlain promised Parliament "further steps . . . to make good our deficiencies in the shortest possible time." But he was determined to restore confidence so that the armaments race could be throttled. To his sister, Ida, he explained on 22 October: "A lot of people seem to me to be losing their heads and talking and thinking as though Munich had made war more instead of less imminent . . . though there are gaps to fill up we need not believe that we have got to make huge additions to the programmes now being put into operation." He was also at pains to emphasise that "the conciliation part of the policy is just as important as the rearming."

For such reasons Chamberlain balked at reconstructing his government to include Labour party members, or taking Eden back into the cabinet. He feared that this "would sooner or later wreck the policy with which I am identified." He resisted the temptation to call a post-Munich election to secure a mandate for his policies, although he did not entirely rule this out. Likewise he rejected suggestions that it was time for Britain to have ministers of supply and National Service. Should the need lessen, the government would have difficulty disbanding them. Chamberlain also admitted that the only reason he hesitated to make further overtures to Hitler was his fear that such a move might precipitate other resignations from his cabinet. . . .

Were the Guilty Men Truly Guilty?

"Were the Guilty Men truly guilty?" Michael Foot, the last surviving member of the "Cato" triumvirate, asked in 1986. His conviction on the subject remains as firmly rooted as in 1940. He still described Dunkirk as "the most dangerous moment in British history since 1066." He noted that his original interpretation had been reinforced by the endorsement from Churchill in his account of the Second World War. Churchill had indicated that the 1930s showed "how the English-speaking peoples through their unwisdom, carelessness and good nature allowed the wicked to rearm." This confirmed Foot's opinion that "those who wish to know what actually happened in the 1930s, how the nation was so nearly led to its doom, had better stick to rough-and-ready guides like *Guilty Men*."

Throughout the 1960s and the 1970s this advice was ignored by many historians. Instead, research was directed to the limitations imposed on foreign policy and the constraints which precluded any alternative to appeasement: global commitments versus limited military resources, rearmament versus fiscal stability, and limited liability versus a continental commitment. While the motives of the appeasers were being rationalised, the "guilty men" thesis was condemned as untenable, misleading and malicious.

The pendulum of appeasement historiography, with the necessary refinements, must now return closer to the position first trumpeted by "Cato." In hot pursuit of documentary evidence in cabinet, committee and departmental files, historians have put aside as irrelevant issues of morality and the dimension of personality. But inherent in the moral fervour of anti-appeasers as "Cato" was a belief in such Gladstonian notions as "maintaining the principles of European law and peace," and that "however deplorable wars may be . . . there are times when justice, when faith, when the welfare of mankind, require a man not to shrink from the responsibility of undertaking them." Throughout 1938 and 1939 Chamberlain's critics were increasingly united by the conviction that Hitler had returned European inter-state relations to the law of the jungle. It was recognised even more widely after the occupation of Czechoslovakia that peace with Nazi Germany could only be purchased at the expense of other nations. The immorality of such a policy is what forced the Chamberlain cabinet to declare war against Germany in September 1939. And it was that moral outrage, culminating in the Dunkirk disaster, which consumed the authors of *Guilty Men* and impelled them to indict the Chamberlain government with such passion. To ignore this dimension in favour of official government documentation is to turn a blind eye to the divisiveness of appeasement. To return to *Guilty Men* is to admit that moral judgments cannot be ignored as "Cato" realised in 1940.

What further compels this move is the evidence contained in the private papers of Neville Chamberlain. An examination of this archive should remind historians how far afield they have strayed from Chamberlain's reality in the 1930s. Chamberlain's papers also confirm many of the original accusations popularised by "Cato." The charges with regard to rearmament appear to be appropriate. This is not to support the view, never maintained by "Cato," that the British government failed to rearm. Rather that deterrence in peace, and defensive rearmament in war, neither deterred nor defended. They certainly failed to meet the requirements of Hitler's *Blitzkrieg*. In that context, Dunkirk was an appropriate outcome to an inappropriate policy.

Closely related is the evidence with regard to the management of public opinion on the issue of military preparedness. Chamberlain's concern was to insure adequate defensive forces to constitute a credible military deterrent to Germany. His confidence in his foreign policy, and its prospects for success, was bolstered by the limited measures of rearmament achieved while he was Prime Minister, and so he informed public opinion on numerous occasions. Self-deception, therefore, rather than the wilful deceit suggested by "Cato," is a more accurate charge, for which there is adequate support.

In the area of foreign policy, denunciation of appeasement permeates every page of *Guilty Men*. What emerges from the evidence in the Chamberlain papers is misplaced trust, unwarranted optimism and erroneous judgments. Confidence in the ultimate success of appeasement or the chances of a negotiated end to the war hindered Chamberlain's assessment of alternatives. On 20 July

1940, after considering reports of a speech by Hitler, Chamberlain accused the *Führer* of "self-deception" and "thinking in blinkers." The same charge of tunnel vision, inherent in *Guilty Men*, equally applied to the British Prime Minister.

Finally, there is abundant evidence that Chamberlain despaired of the political talent at his disposal either in the cabinet or among younger Conservative members of Parliament. Ironically, in that he differed little from "Cato." The lack of political talent served to consolidate the Chamberlain one-man-band approach to foreign policy. It strengthened Chamberlain's convictions as to the appropriateness of his policies and his indispensability. For these reasons he could never contemplate the prospect of failure with equanimity.

Foreign policy, in the final analysis, is judged equally by justice and success. Appeasement, which was intended to conciliate, failed to pacify. Rearmament, which was meant to deter, failed to do so. War, which it was hoped to avoid, broke out on 3 September 1939, and the British Expeditionary Force proved inadequate for its task. As Michael Foot observed, "often the guilty men have seemed to offer evidence against themselves."

Roy Douglas

Chamberlain Attempted the Impossible

In contrast to Professor Aster, Roy Douglas of the University of Surrey, Great Britain, argues that Chamberlain was guilty only of failing to save the peace. The fundamental problems that threatened it were not of his causing, and he carried out a realistic policy—perhaps the only policy possible—that simply could not be made to work in the economic and political climate of the latter 1930s. Chamberlain played as best he could the losing hand dealt him: "It does him no dishonour," Douglas concludes, "that he made the attempt."

Criticism of Chamberlain's foreign policy is often posited on the grounds that the whole idea of "appeasement" towards the "dictators" was wrong from the outset. Part of the trouble here, as we have already seen, stems from confusion as to what the word "appeasement" meant, at least before 1938, to the people who used it. Some critics, however, seem to have taken the much more radical view that the whole idea of securing some kind of *détente* with "dictators" was wrong *ab initio*.

It is perhaps pertinent to ask who were the "dictators." If by the word "dictator" we mean a person in whose hands a very large degree of executive power is concentrated, then in 1938 most states in Europe were dictatorships, and every one of the European states which proponents of the "Grand Alliance" sought to link with Britain and France in defence of Czechoslovakia was undeniably a dictatorship. The "dictators," however, were usually taken to mean Hitler and Mussolini, with perhaps Franco added. This view is really an extraordinary one; for, beyond doubt, Stalin in particular possessed a far greater concentration of executive power than Mussolini or even Hitler. His record of treatment of political opponents before 1938 was incomparably more vicious than that of any man in the world. It is sometimes forgotten that the worst horrors of Hitler's régime belong to the wartime period. The one aspect in which Stalin appeared objectively preferable to Hitler or Mussolini was that he showed little disposition to attack contiguous states; though whether this useful characteristic was founded in lack of will or in lack of power was a matter of speculation at the time, and the answer is today known all too well. Many people seem to have had a curious set of double standards when they discussed the race of "dictators."

Unless we subscribe to these double standards, it is difficult to escape the conclusion that the policy of "appeasement" in the original sense was about the most sensible course to follow in the world which Chamberlain found when he took office in 1937. The balance of forces was changing very rapidly, and the post-war political settlement was bound to be challenged. As that challenge was inevitable, then surely it was better that the changes should be brought about peacefully through negotiations, rather than by war or blatant threat of war? If Hitler and Mussolini were in a position to enforce change, then it was wiser to negotiate with them than to await passively the course of events.

If, then, we conclude that Chamberlain made the best of an extremely bad international situation down to mid-March 1938, then the place or places where the fundamental errors were made must be sought in the period before Chamberlain became Prime Minister.

Various dates in the 1930s have been suggested as the turning point, as the last moment when it was possible to halt the course of events which would lead to world war. These dates include the German military occupation of the Rhineland in March 1936; the Italian invasion of Abyssinia in October 1935; the Japanese attack on China which commenced in September 1931. At all of these points, however, the question is the same: Did it lie in the power of a British Government to compel the aggressor to withdraw? It is difficult to see how in any of these cases the answer could be other than negative. Whether Britain was physically in a position to come to grips with the offenders seems doubtful; whether the British people would have countenanced policies which risked war on any of these occasions is even more so. As the Abyssinian episode showed, economic measures were not merely ineffective, they were disastrously counter-productive.

It is not difficult to pick out other occasions in the early 1930s, or in the 1920s, when decisions taken by British politicians increased the danger of war. The firm impression remains, however, that even if that particular war with that particular enemy had been averted, some other major European war would probably have come. The crucial decisions seem to be those taken immediately after the First World War—though for reasons different from those which many critics of "Versailles" have suggested.

In the spring of 1938, when British statesmen were compelled to consider the Sudetenland question as a matter of urgency, they were reminded that the decision to include the territory within Czechoslovakia was originally taken partly for economic reasons: in order to balance the mainly agricultural Slav regions with a predominantly industrial area. Why, we may ask, was this considered necessary? Why should the Great Powers, or the Czechs themselves, have wished to incorporate a substantial number of people with a very different language and culture from the majority, when these people could have been included relatively easily in Germany or Austria? There were similar questions in other future trouble-spots. There was not the slightest doubt that Danzig was German. Why, then, should the Poles have been anxious that it should become and remain a Free City under the League of Nations, while the Germans were anxious that it should return to the Reich? Why was Memel—also undeniably German—first created a Free City, and later seized by Lithuania?

The answers to all these questions are similar. One of the most fundamental assumptions made by European states in 1919 and thereafter was economic nationalism: the idea that the nation-state should form, so far as possible, a self-contained economic unit, surrounded by tariffs, quotas and other barriers to trade with outsiders. It was important for the Czechs to possess the Sudetenland not only because it was part of historic Bohemia, but also because the Sudetendeutsch would consume the agricultural surplus of Slav peasants, who would encounter difficulties if they attempted to sell across national boundaries. It was also important to the Czechs that the industrial products which they needed could be obtained from within their own economic unit, lest they should be at the mercy of hostile economic policies pursued by foreign governments. It was important to Poland that Danzig should not be German, because it would then be possible for the Germans to impede or tax Polish trade which—until Gdynia was built—had no other convenient channel to the outside world. For similar reasons, it was important for Lithuania to control Memel.

Thus the fundamental weakness of the 1919 settlement was that it failed to tackle the question of economic nationalism: indeed, it made matters even worse than they had been before 1914. In place of the three great Empires of Central and Eastern Europe, the peacemakers set up, or ratified, a mass of states, each determined so far as it could to become economically self-sufficient. Behind the trade barriers erected by those states there grew pressure-groups of capital or labour or both combined, who spoke of "trade wars," or "exporting unemployment," and demanded more trade barriers still. In the end, Germany (and others too) came to dream of wars of conquest, to establish a hegemony over neighbours which would give captive markets to their exporters, and ensure that their own nationals did not suffer from adverse trade policies pursued by outsiders. Britain, the last great Free Trade nation, abandoned her traditional policy piecemeal during the inter-war period, making the final break in 1932 with the general imposition of tariffs. This served as a most baleful example to others. Neville Chamberlain, the "Appeasement" Prime Minister of 1938, was attempting to cope with a political situation which was to a large extent the fault of Neville Chamberlain, the "Protectionist" Chancellor of the Exchequer of 1932.

Although the situation which Chamberlain tried to meet in 1938 had causes which were largely economic, it was no longer possible by that time to administer an economic cure—or, indeed, any cure at all. Too many interests, too many emotions, had been engaged on all sides. We have already had cause to note how in 1938 many of the older and wealthier Germans felt the gravest apprehensions about political expansion which carried the risk of war; but their counsels had been swept aside by others who were stirred by emotions which were largely non-economic in character.

This argument, in its most extreme form, could lead us not merely to the view that there was no chance of saving peace in 1938, but to the conclusion that the 1919 "settlement," or the economic policies of the very early 1930s, would have led to the Second World War, even if Hitler, Mussolini and Stalin had all never lived. There may be a germ of truth in that; but the present author contends for a milder proposition. The policies of economic nationalism sowed the dragon's teeth; but it was not certain that they would germinate and the armed men spring forth. As the years advanced, the danger increased, and the measure of statesmanship required to avert that war also increased. By 1938—probably several years before—the prospect of preserving peace was negligibly small. Neville Chamberlain failed because he attempted the impossible; but it does him no dishonour that he made the attempt.

A. J. P. Taylor

A Triumph for All That Was Best in British Life

In one of the best known excerpts from perhaps the most controversial book on the origins of the Second World War, the late A. J. P. Taylor argued that Munich was in many ways a success for the British belief in fair play and opposition to the harshness of the Treaty of Versailles and not the blundering into a trap laid by Hitler. In contrast to the critique and defense of the last two selections, Taylor suggested that Chamberlain made the case for Munich in the wrong terms—by arguing, for example, that Britain could not respond militarily—and

Britons and Germans alike drew the correspondingly wrong lessons from it—that Britain must rearm more thoroughly or that force was all that mattered. Therefore: "What was done at Munich mattered less than the way it was done."

The conference at Munich was meant to mark the beginning of an epoch in European affairs. "Versailles"—the system of 1919—was not only dead, but buried. A new system, based on equality and mutual confidence between the four great European Powers, was to take its place. Chamberlain said: "I believe that it is peace for our time"; Hitler declared: "I have no more territorial demands to make in Europe." There were still great questions to be settled in international affairs. The Spanish civil war was not over. Germany had not recovered her colonies. More remotely, agreements would have to be reached over economic policy and over armaments, before stability was restored in Europe. None of these questions threatened to provoke a general war. The demonstration had been given that Germany could attain by peaceful negotiation the position in Europe to which her resources entitled her. The great hurdle had been successfully surmounted: the system, directed against Germany, had been dismantled by agreement, without a war. Yet, within six months, a new system was being constructed against Germany. Within a year, Great Britain, France, and Germany were at war. Was "Munich" a fraud from the start—for Germany merely a stage in the march towards world conquest, or, on the side of Great Britain and France, merely a device to buy time until their re-armament was more advanced? So it appeared in retrospect. When the policy of Munich failed, everyone announced that he had expected it to fail; and the participants not only accused the others of cheating, but boasted that they had been cheating themselves. In fact, no one was as clear-sighted as he later claimed to have been; and the four men of Munich were all in their different ways sincere, though each had reserves which he concealed from the others.

The French yielded most, and with least hope for the future. They surrendered the position of paramount European power which they had appeared to enjoy since 1919. But what they surrendered was artificial. They yielded to reality rather than to force. . . .

The British position was more complicated. Morality did not enter French calculations, or entered only to be discarded. The French recognised that it was their duty to assist Czechoslovakia; they rejected this duty as either too dangerous or too difficult. Léon Blum expressed French feeling best when he welcomed the agreement of Munich with a mixture of shame and relief. With the British, on the other hand, morality counted for a great deal. The British statesmen used practical arguments: the danger from air attack; the backwardness of their re-armament; the impossibility, even if adequately armed, of helping Czechoslovakia. But these arguments were used to reinforce morality, not to silence it. British policy over Czechoslovakia originated in the belief that Germany had a moral right to the Sudeten German territory, on grounds of national principle; and it drew the further corollary that this victory for self-determination would provide a stabler, more permanent peace in Europe. The British government were not driven to acknowledge the dismemberment of Czechoslovakia solely from fear of war. They deliberately set out to impose this cession of territory on the Czechs before the threat of war raised its head. The settlement at Munich was a triumph for British policy, which had worked precisely to this end; not a triumph for Hitler, who had started with no such clear intention. Nor was it merely a triumph for selfish or cynical British statesmen, indifferent to the fate of far-off peoples or calculating that Hitler might be launched into war against Soviet Russia. It was a triumph for all that was best and most enlightened in British life; a triumph for those who had preached equal justice between peoples; a triumph for those who had courageously denounced the harshness and short-sightedness of Versailles. Brailsford, the leading Socialist authority on foreign affairs, wrote in 1920 of the peace settlement: "The worst offence was the subjection of over three million Germans to Czech rule." This was the offence redressed at Munich. Idealists could claim that British policy had been tardy and hesitant. In 1938 it atoned for these failings. With skill and persistence, Chamberlain brought first the French, and then the Czechs, to follow the moral line.

There was a case against ceding Sudeten territory to Germany—the case that economic and geographic ties are more important than those of nationality. This had been the case against breaking up the Habsburg Monarchy; the Czechs who had taken the lead in breaking up the Monarchy could not use this argument, nor could their advocates in Western Europe. The dispute had to be transferred from the field of morality to that of practical considerations—to what is disapprovingly called *realpolitik*. The most outspoken opponents of Munich, such as Winston Churchill, asserted quite simply that Germany was becoming too powerful in Europe and that she must be stopped by the threat of a great coalition or, if necessary, by force of arms. Self-determination—the principle to which Czechoslovakia owed her existence—was dismissed as a sham. The only moral argument used was that the frontiers of existing states were sacred and that each state could behave as it liked within its own borders. This was the argument of legitimacy; the argument of Metternich and the Congress of Vienna. If accepted, it would have forbidden not only the break-up of the Habsburg Monarchy, but even the winning of independence by the British colonies in America. It was a strange argument for the British Left to use in 1938; and it sat uneasily upon them—hence the hesitations and ineffectiveness of their criticism. Duff Cooper, First Lord of the Admiralty, had no such doubts when he resigned in protest against the Munich settlement. As became an admiring biographer of Talleyrand, he was concerned with the Balance of Power and British honour, not with self-determination or the injustices of Versailles. For him, Czechoslovakia had no more been the real issue in 1938 than Belgium had been in 1914. This argument destroyed the moral validity of the British position in the First World War, but it had an appeal for the Conservative majority in the House of Commons. Chamberlain had to answer it in its own terms of power. He could not stress the unwillingness of the French to fight, which had been the really decisive weakness on the Western side. Therefore he had to make out that Great Britain herself was in no position to fight Germany.

Chamberlain was caught by his own argument. If Great Britain had been too weak to fight, then the government must speed rearmament; and this involved doubt in Hitler's good faith, whether avowed or not. In this way, Chamberlain did more than anyone else to destroy the case for his own policy. Moreover, one suspicion breeds another. It is doubtful whether Hitler ever took Chamberlain's sincerity seriously before Munich; it is certain that he did not do so a few days afterwards. What was meant as appeasement had turned into capitulation, on Chamberlain's own showing. Hitler drew the lesson that threats were his most potent weapon. The temptation to boast of Munich as a triumph of force was too great to be resisted. Hitler no longer expected to make gains by parading his grievances against Versailles; he expected to make them by playing on British and French fears. Thus he confirmed the suspicions of those who attacked Munich as a craven surrender. International morality was at a discount. Paradoxically, Benes was the true victor of Munich in the long run. For, while Czechoslovakia lost territory and later her independence also, Hitler lost the moral advantage which had hitherto made him irresistible. Munich became an emotive word, a symbol of shame, about which men can still not speak dispassionately. What was done at Munich mattered less than the way in which it was done; and what was said about it afterwards on both sides counted for still more.

Paul Kennedy

Appeasement and Its Interpreters

In considering the gulf between the "guilty men" interpretation of appeasement and the opposing view so forcefully exemplified by A. J. P. Taylor, Paul Kennedy, J. Richardson Dilworth Professor of History at Yale University, argues that simply to condemn the appeasers in moral terms or, on the other hand, to defend them without consideration for their errors is ultimately unproductive.

From "Appeasement," in Gordon Martel, ed., *The Origins of the Second World War Reconsidered*, 1986, pp. 155–157. Published by Unwin Hyman Ltd.

As noted above, the weakness of the older "guilty men" literature upon appeasement appeared to be that it denounced Chamberlain and his colleagues for a failure of morality and willpower *without* much appreciation (or knowledge) of the difficulties under which British governments of the 1920s and 1930s labored. By contrast, most of the later works have focused upon the seemingly compelling strategic, economic and political motives behind British policy at that time, but *without* much concern for the moral and ideological aspects of it. That is to say, the mass of cool Treasury memoranda and the well-honed strategic assessments of the Chiefs of Staff, available for everyone to see in the Public Record Office, now occupy such a prominent position in the story that they are in danger of overshadowing those very important personal feelings behind appeasement: the contempt and indifference felt by many leading Englishmen towards east-central Europe, the half-fear/half-admiration with which Nazi Germany and fascist Italy were viewed, the detestation of communism, the apprehensions about future war.

Of course the warnings of the Treasury and the Chiefs of Staff about Britain's impending financial and strategical bankruptcy were important; but the fact is that such statements were not infallible, and that they *were* sometimes used by Chamberlain to justify policies he already wanted to pursue. For example, as Correlli Barnett and Williamson Murray have pointed out, both the Chiefs of Staff and the Cabinet were making some excessively gloomy predictions during the Czech crisis. Germany's own weaknesses were not considered. The value of the Czech army was ignored. Britain's vulnerability to aerial attack was repeatedly stressed, but without consideration of whether the *Luftwaffe* would or could throw itself against London whilst Germany was engaged in a central European war. Furthermore, the Cabinet minutes reveal that when some ministers (Duff Cooper, Stanley) actually wanted to take a stronger stand against Hitler despite the risks to Britain and its empire, they were swiftly overwhelmed by counter-arguments from Chamberlain and his friends: objectors within the Cabinet had to be silenced, just as the press and BBC had to be controlled. Even when, by early-to-mid 1939, British public opinion was moving strongly against appeasement, when Britain's aerial defenses were much improved, and when the dominions were more supportive of a firm line, Chamberlain and his fellow-appeasers were still seeking, in secret rather than in the open, to buy off Hitler. After Prague, making concessions to Germany was neither as logical nor as "natural" as it might have been in 1936 and 1926; on the contrary, it seemed to many a policy lacking both in practical wisdom *and* moral idealism. Yet it was still being attempted by Downing Street, which suggests that individual convictions—in this case, Chamberlain's—must play a central part in our explanation of British policy, and that it cannot be fully understood simply in terms of "objective" strategical and economic realities.

Appeasement, then, is not a simple phenomenon which can be defined in a few, sharp words. Older histories tend to see it as a shameful and bankrupt policy of surrender to the dictator-states. Taylor has portrayed it as a well-meaning series of bungles which eventually embroiled both Hitler and the West in a war neither of them desired. Some scholars have seen it as a natural and rational strategy in the light of Britain's weaknesses in the world by the 1930s. Others have pointed out that it was, albeit in a more intensified form, a normal continuation of the British diplomatic tradition of attempting to settle disputes peacefully.

Appeasement was, in fact, all of the above and needs to be understood as such. It also needs to be investigated at different levels of causality, so that distinctions can be made between the nebulous, sometimes confused mentality of the appeasers on the one hand, and the cluster of military or economic or imperial or domestic-political motives which justified (or seemed to justify) concessions to the dictators on the other. Only when it is approached in such a way will the historians rise above the simplistic, one-dimensional descriptions, and deal with appeasement as the complex, variegated, shifting phenomenon which it really was.

Keith Middlemas

Reckoning

Keith Middlemas, professor of history at the University of Sussex, Great Britain, writes that although the Chamberlain policy of appeasement was a genuine attempt to bring British commitments into line with British power, it is not correct to excuse the failure of appeasement by declaring that the problems facing it were too formidable. There were, he suggests, several clearly definable errors in the Chamberlain foreign policy that negated any hope of success.

Since 1918, Britain had been continuously in search of a foreign policy where her obligations and resources would balance. Only at certain moments, in the four years after Locarno, and perhaps in the brief glow after Stresa in 1935, did she manage to discover one. But an attempt was made, in 1937–9, to bring commitments and power into alignment, and Chamberlain's Government may be commended for its realistic acceptance of Britain's diminished estate in relation to the rest of the world. . . .

Nevertheless, the criticisms made here of British foreign policy are valid. If the Chamberlain Government regarded the security of France as an essential interest–as it showed in January and March 1939—then the previous lack of liaison and their high-handed treatment of their ally was unwise and probably deeply harmful. Britain bears a heavy share of responsibility for undermining the will of France to resist. Secondly, a charge which can be explained but not excused, the British deliberately refused to envisage Russia as an ally, rebuffed what, on the evidence available, appear to have been genuine overtures and alienated the Soviet government so far that the negotiations of 1939 were crippled before they began. A country in Britain's position cannot afford to choose only those allies with whom it is in sympathy. Thirdly, the extreme degree of isolationism ceased to make sense when reduced to strategic terms.

From *The Strategy of Appeasement: The British Government and Germany*, Quadrangle Books, 1972, pp. 453–457. Published by Weidenfeld & Nicolson Ltd.

The building-up of a fighter and radar defence screen and a navy capable of preventing a German invasion indicated a policy of withdrawal from Europe, yet the British patently relied on France to hold the Western front on land and to provide reinforcements for Britain in the air. Without offering a field force in return, the expectation of French altruism was remarkable. The counter argument, that the fighter screen enabled Britain to defeat the German attack in 1940, ignores the possibility that, if a proper Field Force had been provided at the beginning, the Battle of Britain might not have occurred. The saddest comment on the reordering of defence priorities in 1937 is the lamentable state of ARP [Air Raid Precautions] and home air defence at the time of Munich. Even the strategy of withdrawal was handled ineptly.

Finally, the Government may be condemned for the way in which the Foreign Office and military experts were overridden or sidetracked—not because this is wrong in itself but because the results were poor and the principle behind it was unsound. A profit-and-loss account of any political project is hard enough to draw up a generation later, with the benefit of more sophisticated techniques of accounting. To attempt to cost the national interest in 1938 was undesirable and probably impossible. The foreign policy of a nation depends on commercial, industrial, military and manpower strength. Without these it carries weight only so long as it is not challenged. In 1938, by throwing too much light, Chamberlain helped to reveal how thin British pretensions were.

The wider question, whether these two years were wholly retrograde or not, is hard to answer since it depends on judgments about alternatives and the historical inevitability of the war. The Eden-Baldwin policy, if it had been continued after 1936, might have advanced through deterrence the sort of stalemate created since the 1950s by nuclear stockpiles. It might also have led to tacit acknowledgement of spheres of influence. Alternatively, after 1936, the British Government *could* have withdrawn into total isolation, by allowing Hitler to dominate the Continent, defeat France, overrun south-eastern Europe and, perhaps, Russia. It might have been possible then to come to a settlement without having to defend the Empire against another German onslaught and to have maintained British trade by skilled negotiation, like the seventeenth-century diplomacy of the Venetian republic when the Doges' real power had gone. To do so would have involved a break with traditions at least 400 years old and, if the example of Venice is taken, a steady reduction in status and final extinction at the hands of the unsentimental. The choice was impossible so long as Britain aspired to great-power status and so long as her Government recognised an interest in the survival of France.

Preventive war was not an option available in the context of British public opinion, but after the crisis of May 1938 the Government could have emphasised, rather than undermined its firmness and warned the British public as well as Germany. As Churchill said, in answer to the question, would he have gone to meet Hitler? "Yes, but I would have invited Hitler to come and meet me in the North Sea on board a British battleship." Creation of a "grand alliance," encouragement of the German resistance to Hitler, and accelerated rearmament after May 1938 might have induced Hitler to abandon the plan to invade Czechoslovakia. To postulate a détente would be to go too far, given the evidence of Hitler's long-term plans, but the limited success suggested by the May crisis might have provided the occasion for a fundamental reappraisal of British policy towards dictators.

Yet this still evades the question about the inevitability of war. If Britain had prepared to mobilise and promised full support to France in August 1938, Hitler might have backed down. On the evidence of his intentions given here, Germany was more likely to fight. Debates about what might have happened usually ignore the likelihood that Germany would have acted otherwise in other contingencies, and there is much to be said for the point put by Chamberlain and Nevile Henderson that warnings repeated too often would ultimately be seen as bluff. In 1938, Britain came near to fulfilling the role Hitler had cast for her, without success. The alternative—that war was preferable then, rather than in 1939—was a difficult if not impossible choice, for in that case the Government would have had to make in peacetime all the decisions normal in time of war. They would have had to win consent for full rearmament, subordination of the economy to war priorities, the introduction of national service and conscription, war budgets and cuts in welfare services, the conversion of industry, the raising of taxation and foreign loans, the sale of overseas investments. By the skilful use of propaganda they might have succeeded, but such mobilisation had never been done in peacetime and during the First World War it had taken nearly two years from August 1914 to convert Britain into an armed camp. Not even Lord Beaverbrook, later the most sanguine exponent of the use of indoctrination, would have found it easy to convert the public, Press and Parliament in 1938.

Is democracy then the scapegoat? Must Britain have been, as Baldwin used to say, two years behind the dictators? (As Cadogan minuted, in November 1938, "national disunity *is* democracy.") Was it possible by 1938, as Churchill had pleaded earlier, that "there need be no talk of working up public opinion. You must not go and ask the public what they think about this"? There was no demand. Churchill himself was in broad agreement with the Government over its policy towards Czechoslovakia until the summer of 1938. None of the political "rebels" disagreed. Even the Labour Party leaders showed themselves more worried about Spain. Czechoslovakia was a question which aroused something as near to a national consensus of opinion as any issue in the 1930s—until Munich.

The six months after Munich are the real test. Until then, a better case can be made out for Chamberlain and his Cabinet than is usually done. It is hard to see that Eden's alternative policy would have accomplished more; and Chamberlain's might conceivably have achieved the Anglo-German détente, if put into effect early in 1937 rather than a year later. Taken at its original, pre-Munich level, Chamberlain's intention may be expressed as coexistence on the basis of separate spheres of influence, a conception as modern as the deterrent-based foreign policy of the Baldwin Government. He might well have succeeded with Mussolini or Stalin, or Goering if he had come to power on the shoulders of the German opposition. To say this, however, is not to excuse the failure to take stock after Munich, nor the inability to educate the British public.

Politicians do not need to accept the limits imposed by their own definitions of public opinion nor make them the excuse for inaction. They do not need to look for simple total solutions which may be easy blind alleys. They do not need to work on unquestioned assumptions, lulled by the stifling wind of approval around them. There is a category of spiritual strength which is not accounted for in statistics. The public, too, have their responsibility, so long as they are informed. If the choice is between guns and butter, they must accept that it is a choice, and make it if the chance is given. But Chamberlain ignored advice to call an election after Munich from colleagues who wanted "national unity" as well as mere party advantage. This, with the admission that Munich was a bare escape from the pit, followed by the preparations eventually made in March 1939, might have saved more than that Government's reputation.

July 1945: Churchill, Truman, and Stalin at Potsdam on the eve of the Cold War. (Interphoto Pressebild Agentur)

PART

The Search for Lessons

Christopher Layne

The Munich Myth and American Foreign Policy

Christopher Layne considers in the following selection the impact on post–Second World War American policymakers of the powerful mythography of Munich and appeasement. Since the Second World War it has been at once a warning and a burden. In the latter years of this century, he suggests, the "lessons of Munich" cannot be allowed to prevent settlements with rivals by forever reinforcing the inclination toward confrontation in the effort to prevent the appearance of appease-

From "The Munich Myth and American Foreign Policy," in Kenneth M. Jensen and David Hendrickson, eds., *The Meaning of Munich Fifty Years Later*, 1990, pp. 13–21. Washington, D.C.: The United States Institute of Peace.

ment. The reader should consider the weight of these remarks—written as the Soviet Union was breaking up—in the context of a post–Cold War world.

Since the end of World War II, American foreign policy has been profoundly influenced by the Munich analogy, or "lesson." It is not unusual that a pivotal historical event should shape the outlook of policymakers years after its occurrence; statesmen and international political analysts have always used historical analogies to help them make sense of the present and predict the future. However, history's lessons must be used cautiously. As political scientist Robert Jervis has observed, historical analogies can be misleading if not used rigorously; too often, attention is paid to what happened rather than to why it happened. The Munich analogy is a case in point; American statesmen have been led astray by applying a "lesson of the past" that at best is a caricature of the events that transpired in 1938.

The Munich Analogy

The accepted wisdom is that Munich signified British Prime Minister Neville Chamberlain's craven capitulation to German Chancellor Adolf Hitler's demands for occupation of Czechoslovakia's German-speaking Sudetenland border area. By yielding, the British (and their French allies) sealed the fate of Czechoslovakia as an independent state and further fueled Hitler's insatiable appetite for conquest. It is widely believed that by firmly supporting Prague, the British and French could have forced Hitler to back down; such a humiliation might have emboldened the German army to overthrow him. And even if the Western powers' firmness had led to war in 1938, the ensuing conflict would have been briefer and less costly than the world war that broke out in the fall of 1939. Thus, in the United States, the generally accepted view is that Munich was the culmination of five years of folly—half a decade in which the British remained blind to the German threat while ignoring the important role of military power in foreign policy.

Munich is a powerful symbol, and myths often exert a greater hold over people's minds than facts. Nevertheless, to be understood properly, history cannot be read backwards. To understand why Britain acted as it did during the 1933–1938 period, one must view the world as it was seen by statesmen at the time. This task is facilitated by the volume of historical research on the origins of World War II that was stimulated by the opening of the British government's archives in the early 1970s. Regrettably, outside a narrow circle of diplomatic historians, the work of English historians remains mostly unknown in the United States. Thus, although based on a false image of history, the Munich analogy still influences many within the American foreign policy community.

Great Britain is the 1930s was a badly fragmented society. The political and class polarizations inflamed by the 1926 general strike and the 1931 financial crisis were still deep and bitter. The British Left regarded the ruling national government with contempt, hostility, and suspicion. Through most of the 1930s, the Left opposed rearmament, conscription, and economic mobilization. Yet, in a curious paradox, the Left supported "collective security" (through the League of Nations) against the fascist dictators while denying the British government the military means to make such a policy credible. Moreover, all segments of British society had been traumatized by the appalling casualties of World War I. As a result, many Britons rejected the very concept of balance-of-power politics, and few were anxious to plunge into another European war. Politicians like Chamberlain, who wanted to press for rearmament, could not ignore these realities. (Fearing it would lead to defeat, Prime Minister Stanley Baldwin rejected Chamberlain's suggestion that the government base the 1935 general election on the issue of rearmament.)

Abroad, Britain had many interests and few reliable allies. At the same time, there were several important threats to British security, of which Germany was simply the most predominant. In the Far East, Japan menaced Australia, New Zealand, and Britain's extensive imperial holdings in China and Southeast Asia. London believed (correctly, it turned out) that Japan would take advantage of an Anglo-German war to move against Britain in the Pacific. Britain's decision to support sanctions by the League of Nations against Italy (in retaliation for the latter's 1935 invasion of Ethiopia) transformed Rome from potential membership in an anti-German coalition into a posture of hostility. This change was important because Italy's not inconsiderable naval power could cut the vital Mediterranean/Suez Canal communications link between the British Isles, India, and the Far East. The dominant strategic reality for British policymakers in the 1930s was that an Anglo-German war would lead almost certainly to a three-front war in which England would also have to fight Japan and Italy.

To meet these dangers, London could count on little help from abroad. During the 1930s, France was wracked by political instability and social turmoil. And while its armed forces looked impressive on paper, the British were skeptical of the French army's capabilities, morale, and equipment. The Soviet Union was understandably viewed with deep suspicion, and its political motives were distrusted. Stalin's purge of the Red Army officer corps, which began in 1937, was thought to negate Soviet military power. For its part, the United States remained steadfastly isolationist. Moreover, the Neutrality Act seemed to foreclose Britain from purchasing war materials or raising loans from the United States during wartime. Finally, the British Dominions (Australia, Canada, New Zealand, and South Africa) wished to remain aloof from European politics and contributed little to the British Empire's defense.

In the 1930s, Britain was the paradigmatic example of an imperially overstretched great power; it simply lacked the resources to provide adequately against the triple threat to its vital interests. London also faced tough decisions about "guns or butter"; these were made even more difficult by the prevailing class antagonisms. Moreover, rearmament required the importation of large quantities of raw materials. These materials had to be paid for by Britain's export income, but the key export industries were also vital war industries. Diverting manufacturing plants from exports to war materials had the perverse effect of making it more difficult for Britain to pay for rearmament and to maintain intact the nation's financial and industrial strength for war.

The Crisis of 1938

When combined with the specific circumstances of 1938, the bleak, constraining circumstances in which London found itself explain why it acted as it did during the Munich crisis. That crisis actually began with the Austrian *Anschluss* in March 1938, which left Czechoslovakia surrounded on three sides by German territory. Obviously, Czechoslovakia would be the next European flash point, and it was equally apparent that Britain could do nothing militarily to prevent Germany from overrunning Czechoslovakia. That unfortunate country could be saved only if the French army took the offensive on the Rhine. The British knew, however, that the French army had neither the plans nor the capability to attack Germany. (Paris admitted as much during the April 1938 Anglo-French staff talks.)

At the outset of the crisis, therefore, London decided it would fight only to maintain the independence of Holland, Belgium, and France; Czechoslovakia was not considered a vital British interest. London's position was communicated to Paris, Berlin, and Prague. London was determined to work toward a peaceful settlement of the Sudeten question that would lead to Germany's annexation of Czechoslovakia's German-speaking borderlands. However, the British warned Berlin repeatedly that any German attempt to resolve the question forcibly could lead to a wider war; if France came to Czechoslovakia's aid and Germany attacked France, Britain would fight.

It is often suggested that the Western powers would have been better off taking on Hitler in September 1938. Clearly, given the objective strategic conditions at the time, a British decision to back Prague would have been nothing more than a pretext for fighting Germany then rather than later. Whether it would have been to the Western powers' military advantage to fight in 1938 is still a much-debated issue. However, at the time, the British chiefs of staff emphatically advised the government to try to buy additional time for rearmament by settling the Czech crisis peacefully. Similarly, there was little support in the nation or in Parliament for fighting in 1938. Not a single leading British politician—not even the renowned antiappeasers Winston Churchill and Anthony Eden—urged that Britain go to war in Czechoslovakia's defense.

In 1938, the British had many reasons to avoid a showdown; there was still reason to hope that an Anglo-German war could be avoided. At the time of Munich, it was not yet clear that Hitler was unappeasable. The full scope of his ambitions was not apparent. His stated objectives differed little from those of anti-Nazi conservative nationalists like Leipzig Lord Mayor Karl Goerderler and Army Chief of Staff General Ludwig Beck. Moreover, few British leaders were convinced of the justice of the World War I Versailles settlement, and there was considerable sympathy for the view that Austria and the German speakers on Germany's borders should be incorporated into the Reich. Moreover, the Dominions were absolutely opposed to fighting over Czechoslovakia, and a British decision to do so would have ripped the very fabric that bound the British Empire together. Most important, however, Britain's governing elite understood full well the implications of another world war: Britain would be economically bankrupted and would lose her empire; social and political upheaval would affect Britain and Europe; Soviet power would advance westward; and the Eurocentric world would collapse as the United States and the Soviet Union emerged as the leading world powers. . . .

Munich and Postwar Policy

Though it accords little with actual events, there is no question that postwar U.S. policy has been significantly affected by the purported lesson of Munich. For postwar American policymakers, Munich seemed to prove that totalitarian states are insatiably aggressive, that peace is indivisible, that aggression must be resisted everywhere, and that "appeasement" (defined as any substantive diplomatic exchange with a totalitarian power) is always folly. Drawing on the experience of the 1930s, Washington concluded that there was no meaningful distinction between Nazi Germany and Soviet Russia (or between Hitler and Stalin). Given the nature of the adversary, the United States was obligated to use force if necessary to resist communism everywhere.

The Munich analogy has been superimposed on a Wilsonian view of international politics and on a fixed set of assumptions about the nature of world politics in the postwar world. Wilsonianism holds that the world will be peaceful and harmonious only if nondemocratic states (which are taken as inherently bellicose) become democracies (which are inherently pacific). Munich led to the conclusion that America was responsible for imposing world order by transforming the domestic political structures of non-democratic states. Indeed, Munich taught that the United States could be truly secure only in an ideologically congenial international milieu.

Thus Munich also helped shape the view that the world system was bipolar ideologically as well as strategically. . . . Moreover, American policymakers believed that the postwar balance of power was fragile and that all of America's security commitments were interdependent. It was feared that any U.S. strategic setback or failure of resolve would erode U.S. credibility and lead to an adverse shift in the global balance. Indeed, credibility itself came to be seen as a vital interest and was regarded as one of the few things worth fighting for. Time and again, the United States found itself defending "interests" that were viewed as symbolically important, although they were intrinsically worthless (like Vietnam).

The domino theory that has bedeviled postwar U.S. foreign policy was rooted in Munich's lesson. As Daniel Yergin wrote in *The Shattered Peace*, Munich stood for the proposition "that international events moved in simple chain reactions, that all points on a map were equally close, and that every event was of equal importance." This notion explains why the global containment policy embodied in the Truman and Reagan Doctrines is without obvious limits. Global containment fails to differentiate between vital and peripheral interests. Indeed, it makes no attempt at all to define U.S. interests extrinsically; instead, American interests exist only in relation to perceived threats. Because it assumes that America is threatened by any communist advance, global containment dictates that America must oppose communism everywhere.

Munich bequeathed the United States an ideologically and threat-driven foreign policy that inexorably led to American involvement in Third World quagmires and U.S. "imperial overstretch." Moreover, as Thomas A. Paterson notes in *Meeting the Communist Threat*, the Munich lesson "put a damper on diplomacy." As he says, "American officials were hesitant to negotiate with an opponent variously described as malevolent, deceitful, and inhuman. They especially did not warm to negotiations when some critics were ready to cry that diplomacy, which could produce compromises, was evidence in itself of softness toward Communism." As George F. Kennan, then Director of the State Department's Policy Planning staff, observed in the late 1940s, these inhibitions on U.S.-Soviet diplomacy may have resulted in a missed opportunity for both superpowers to withdraw their forces from Central Europe, resolve the German Question, and prevent the "congealing" of Europe's division.

Moving Beyond Munich

Fifty years after Munich, the United States and the Soviet Union seem poised for a dramatic breakthrough in their relationship. The improved climate of superpower relations is traceable to several factors. First, the relative power of both the United States and the Soviet Union has declined (albeit for different reasons). As a result, Washington and Moscow are both looking for ways to shed international burdens and divert more resources to pressing domestic problems. Moreover, under Mikhail Gorbachev, Soviet foreign policy has changed in key respects. Moscow appears to have concluded that in the Third World, the game of great-power competition is not worth the cost and that its Third World allies subtract from Soviet strength rather than add to it. In the strategic area, new thinking by the Soviets about mutual security and defensive sufficiency is an encouraging development. Soviet views of international relations appear to be changing too, and Moscow appears to be abandoning the belief that world politics is a struggle between classes or social systems.

In coming years, there may be heretofore unimaginable diplomatic opportunities in U.S.-Soviet relations. The Soviet withdrawal from Afghanistan, Kremlin hints that both superpowers weigh anchor and leave Central Europe, and intimations that the Soviet Union has repealed the Brezhnev Doctrine and is prepared to accept pluralism in Eastern Europe should all be tested by constructive American initiatives. For the first time since the 1945–1948 period, the mutual disengagement of both superpowers from Central Europe may be a serious possibility. Such an agreement would radically reduce the chances of war in Europe by lowering political tensions, thus helping ensure that Eastern Europe does not become the Sarajevo of the 1990s. Both superpowers have an interest in "Finlandizing" Eastern Europe by reconciling legitimate Soviet security concerns with Eastern Europe's desire for greater autonomy and for political and economic reform. Mutual disengagement would also bolster Western Europe's security.

It would be tragic if the United States failed to fully explore this possibility because it clung to the view—rooted in the Munich analogy—that it is impossible to negotiate with the Soviet Union. It is time American policymakers realize that Soviet Russia is not Nazi Germany. The Soviet Union has followed a cautious, risk-adverse, traditional great-power foreign policy. No doubt the Soviets expand their influence when the costs and risks of doing so are small. But the Soviet Union is not insatiably aggressive, and the U.S. policy of containment has demonstrated that the Soviets are unwilling to risk war with the United States to expand their international power position. Certainly, Soviet leaders (including, in the sphere of foreign policy, Stalin) have not been like Hitler.

The U.S.-Soviet relationship is one of ambiguity; the superpowers are great power rivals, but they have congruent as well as conflicting interests. It is time to move beyond the Munich myth. As Walter Lippmann said, "The history of diplomacy is the history of relations among rival powers, which did not enjoy political intimacy. . . . Nevertheless there have been political settlements. . . . For a diplomat to think that rival and unfriendly powers cannot be brought to settlement is to forget what diplomacy is all about."

Suggestions for Additional Reading

The literature on the subject of British appeasement reflects the interest of historians in the subject: simply put, it is truly enormous. Readers of this collection are reminded that virtually all of the books noted below contain general or specialized bibliographies that are invaluable guides. In addition, the bibliographic essays by Donald Cameron Watt, "The Historiography of Appeasement," in Alan Sked and Chris Cook, eds., *Crisis and Controversy: Essays in Honour of A. J. P. Taylor* (London, 1976), and by Paul Kennedy, "Appeasement," in Gordon Martel, ed., *The Origins of the Second World War Reconsidered* (Boston, 1986), are models of the type. Also not to be missed is the thorough bibliography compiled by Sidney Aster, *British Foreign Policy, 1918–1945* (Wilmington, 1984). What follows is a discussion of a number of the most significant works on the subject, some featured in these three bibliographic essays and others not, which are useful to students.

For many years the standard work, still well worth reading, on appeasement and the coming of World War II was Sir John Wheeler-Bennett, *Munich: Prologue to Tragedy* (New York, 1963 ed.). It has been joined by many others, including Martin Gilbert and Richard Gott, *The Appeasers* (New York, 1963); also by Martin Gilbert is *The Roots of Appeasement* (New York, 1966). Other general works dealing with the appeasement period are: Sidney Aster, *1939: The Making of the Second World War* (London, 1973); Maurice Baumont, *The Origins of the Second World War* (New Haven, 1978); Maurice Cowling, *The Impact of Hitler* (Cambridge, 1975); Keith Eubank, *Munich* (Norman, 1963); Donald Lammers, *Explaining Munich* (Stanford, 1966); Keith Middlemas, *The Strategy of Appeasement: The British Government and Germany* (Chicago, 1972); Wolfgang J. Mommsen and Lothar Kettenacker, eds., *The Fascist Challenge and the Policy of Appeasement* (London, 1984); Richard Overy and Andrew Wheatcroft, *The Road to War* (London, 1989); William R. Rock, *British Appeasement in the*

1930's (Hamden, Connecticut, 1977); and by the same author, *Appeasement on Trial: British Foreign Policy and Its Critics* (Hamden, Connecticut, 1966); also Keith Robbins, *Munich, 1938* (London, 1968); Telford Taylor, *Munich: The Price of Peace* (New York, 1979); and Richard Lamb, *The Ghosts of Peace, 1935–1945* (Salisbury, U. K., 1987). The most recent work in this category is R. J. Q. Adams, *British Politics and Foreign Policy in the Age of Appeasement, 1935–39* (Stanford, 1992). Among the many interesting relevant collections of essays are David Dilks, ed., *Retreat from Power: Studies in Britain's Foreign Policy in the Twentieth Century* (London, 1981), and Kenneth M. Jensen and David Wurmser, eds., *The Meaning of Munich Fifty Years Later* (Washington, D.C., 1990).

Of particular interest are the controversial works that have defined the polar regions of appeasement studies. First in this category is the work by three then-youthful journalists (Michael Foot, Peter Howard, and Frank Owen) writing under the pen name "Cato," *Guilty Men* (London, 1940). Its brutal, condemnatory language pillories the Baldwin and Chamberlain governments for failing their country. From that time, appeasement books have been either "Guilty Men" books or not. Another famous diatribe of that school is A. L. Rowse, *Appeasement: A Study in Political Decline, 1933–39* (New York, 1961). Perhaps even more controversial is the work by A. J. P. Taylor excerpted in this book, *The Origins of the Second World War* (New York, 1968 ed.), which takes the opposite view, arguing that the appeasers could not be guilty of playing into the hands of a warmonger because war was not Hitler's plan at all. The level of feeling over this book is underscored by the fact that two collections of essays about the controversy it sparked have been published: William Roger Louis, ed., *The Origins of the Second World War: A. J. P. Taylor and His Critics* (London, 1971); and the work edited by Gordon Martel, noted above.

A grounding in defense policy in the interwar years may be gained from consulting Peter Dennis, *Decision by Default: Peacetime Conscription and British Defense, 1919–1939* (Durham, North Carolina, 1972); Donald Cameron Watt, *Too Serious a Business: European Armed Forces and the Approach of the Second World War* (London, 1978); Brian Bond, *British Military Policy Between the Two World Wars* (Oxford, 1980); and Michael Howard, *The Conti-*

nental Commitment (London, 1972).

Among the vast literature on the subject of rearmament policy are N. H. Gibbs, *Rearmament Policy* (London, 1976), Vol. I of J. R. M. Butler, ed., *Grand Strategy* in the *British Official History of the Second World War*; G. C. Peden, *British Rearmament and the Treasury, 1932–1939* (Edinburgh, 1979); Robert Paul Shay, *British Rearmament in the Thirties* (Princeton, 1977).

Malcolm Smith, *British Air Strategy Between the Wars* (London, 1984); Paul Haggie, *Britannia at Bay: The Defence of the British Empire Against Japan, 1931–41* (London, 1981); and Stephen Roskill, *Naval Policy Between the Wars, 1919–1939*, 2 vols. (London, 1968, 1976), pay close attention to the various services.

On the question of public opinion and military planning, there are Uri Bialer, *The Shadow of the Bomber: The Fear of Air Attack and British Politics, 1932–1939* (London, 1980), and Patrick Kyba, *Covenants Without Swords: Public Opinion and British Defence Policy* (Waterloo, Ontario, 1983).

Useful on the crises that challenged the appeasers in the 1930s—the infamous steps toward war, as the Churchillians characterized them—are James T. Emmerson, *The Rhineland Crisis, March 7, 1936: A Study in Multilateral Diplomacy* (Ames, Iowa, 1977); Frank Hardie, *The Abyssinian Crisis* (London, 1974); Gordon Brook-Shepherd, *The Anschluss* (Philadelphia, 1963); Jill Edwards, *The British Government and the Spanish Civil War, 1936–1939* (London, 1979); and Bradford A. Lee, *Britain and the Sino-Japanese War, 1937–1939* (Stanford, 1973).

For an understanding of the post-Munich period see the comprehensive study by Donald Cameron Watt, *How War Came* (New York, 1989); and for the decision to guarantee Poland, see Simon Newman, *March 1939: The British Guarantee to Poland* (Oxford, 1976).

Of great importance in understanding appeasement, of course, are the motivations and positions of the statesmen, officials, and diplomats who made, carried out, or opposed the policy. Among the many biographies to be consulted are J. A. Cross, *Sir Samuel Hoare* (London, 1977), and by the same author, *Lord Swinton* (London, 1982); Martin Gilbert, *Winston Churchill, Vol. V: The Prophet of Truth, 1922–1939* (New York, 1976); Keith Middlemas and John Barnes, *Baldwin* (New York, 1970); John Charmley, *Duff Cooper* (London, 1986); and Robert Rhodes James, *Anthony Eden* (London, 1987). More critical of Eden is David Carlton, *Anthony Eden* (London, 1981). Though not precisely a biography, also excellent is A. R. Peters, *Anthony Eden at the Foreign Office* (Aldershot, 1986). Insights into perspectives of the Opposition Labour party may be gained from Alan Bullock, *The Life and Times of Ernest Bevin*, 3 vols. (London, 1960–1983); and Ben Pimlott, *Hugh Dalton* (London, 1985).

Studies of senior civil servant Sir Robert Vansittart, by Ian Colvin, *Vansittart in Office* (London, 1965), and Norman Rose, *Vansittart: Portrait of a Diplomat* (London, 1978); and of Sir Maurice Hankey, by Stephen Roskill, *Hankey: Man of Secrets*, 3 vols. (London, 1970–1974) and John F. Naylor, *A Man and an Institution* (Cambridge, 1984), are enlightening.

Memoirs published years after this period by the principal players who had reputations to repair or protect must, for obvious reasons, be treated with care. With that in mind, one should consult among the many such books Leopold S. Amery, *My Political Life, Vol. III* (London, 1955); Clement R. Attlee, *As It Happened* (London, 1954); the Earl of Avon (Anthony Eden), *Facing the Dictators* (Boston, 1962); Winston S. Churchill, *The Gathering Storm* (New York, 1948); Alfred Duff Cooper, *Old Men Forget* (London, 1953); Hugh Dalton, *The Fateful Years: Memoirs, 1931–1945* (London, 1957); the Earl of Halifax, *Fullness of Days* (New York, 1957); the Earl of Swinton, *I Remember* (London, 1948); and Viscount Templewood (Sir Samuel Hoare), *Nine Troubled Years* (London, 1954). The memoirs of the pro-appeasement British ambassador to Germany during this period, Sir Nevile Henderson, *Failure of a Mission* (London, 1940), are instructive, though not convincing. Recollections by high-ranking civil servants and diplomats include Sir Maurice Peterson, *Both Sides of the Curtain* (London, 1950); Sir Walford Selby, *Diplomatic Twilight, 1930–1950* (London, 1953); Sir William Strang, *Home and Abroad* (London, 1956); and Lord Vansittart (Sir Robert Vansittart), *The Mist Procession* (London, 1958).

Among the published papers of these notables are John Barnes and David Nicolson, eds., *The Empire at Bay: The Leo Amery*

Diaries, 1929–1945 (London, 1988); David Dilks, ed., *The Diaries of Sir Alexander Cadogan, 1938–1945* (London, 1971); John Harvey, ed., *The Diplomatic Diaries of Oliver Harvey* (London, 1970); R. J. Minney, ed., *The Private Papers of Hore-Belisha* (London, 1960); Nigel Nicolson, *Harold Nicolson, Diaries and Letters, 1930–39* (London, 1966). Among the most entertaining diaries published is that of Neville Chamberlain's greatest admirer: Robert Rhodes James, *Chips: The Diaries of Sir Henry Channon* (London, 1967).

Insights into the military thinking of the period can be gained by consulting Sir Basil Liddell Hart, *The Liddell Hart Memoirs, Vol. II* (London, 1965); Roderick MacLeod and Denis Kelly, *The Ironside Diaries, 1937–1940* (London, 1963); Sir John Slessor, *The Central Blue* (London, 1957); and Lord Chatfield, *It Might Happen Again* (London, 1947).

There is no shortage of studies of politics in the appeasement period, and useful among works on the subject are: Stuart Ball, *Baldwin and the Conservative Party* (London, 1988); Correlli Barnett, *The Collapse of British Power* (Gloucester, U.K., 1984 ed.); Donald Birn, *The League of Nations Union, 1918–1945* (London, 1981); Richard Shepherd, *A Class Divided: Appeasement and the Road to Munich, 1938* (London, 1989); John Ramsden, *The Making of Conservative Party Policy: The Conservative Research Department Since 1929* (London, 1980); and Neville Thompson, *The Anti-Appeasers: Conservative Opposition to Appeasement in the 1930s* (London, 1971). Though it deals with the period before Chamberlain's rise to the premiership, worthwhile reading is Gustav Schmidt, *The Politics and Economics of Appeasement* (New York, 1986).

For the press during the period see A. J. P. Taylor, *Lord Beaverbrook* (New York, 1972); Franklin Reid Gannon, *The British Press and Germany, 1936–1939* (London, 1971); and Stephen Koss, *The Rise and Fall of the Political Press in Britain, Vol. II: The Twentieth Century* (Chapel Hill, 1984).

The books that take as their subject the career and personality of Neville Chamberlain constitute a whole subset of appeasement studies. David Dilks has published only the first volume of his projected massive study, *Neville Chamberlain* (Cambridge, 1984); it stops at 1929. The veteran biography of similar title by Sir Keith Feiling (London, 1946) is still the best single-volume life. Also useful (and also taking the same title) is that by H. Montgomery Hyde (London, 1976). Iain Macleod, himself once a Conservative cabinet member, offers a sympathetic view of Chamberlain and his many problems in *Neville Chamberlain* (London, 1962). Chamberlain is always at center stage in: Ian Colvin, *The Chamberlain Cabinet* (London, 1971); John Charmley, *Chamberlain and the Lost Peace* (London, 1989); Richard Cockett, *Twilight of Truth: Chamberlain, Appeasement and the Manipulation of the Press* (London, 1989); Larry William Fuchser, *Neville Chamberlain and Appeasement* (New York, 1982); and William R. Rock, *Chamberlain and Roosevelt* (Columbus, Ohio, 1988).

Most papers of the various departments of state in Great Britain are now open to examination after thirty years, and very few from the appeasement period are still classified. Still in the process of publication are the *Documents on British Foreign Policy* Series II and III (London, 1946–), which offer a broad selection of the documentary evidence of the diplomatic history of the period. Most of the private papers of the principal political and other figures of the appeasement period are also open to scholars.